Table of Contents

Introduction 8

Chapter 1. Understanding Clean Eating 9

Chapter 2: Breakfasts to Start Your Day Right 12
1. Berry and Nut Oatmeal Bowl 12
2. Avocado Toast with Egg and Tomato 13
3. Green Spinach Banana Smoothie 13
4. Quinoa Fruit Salad with Minty Yogurt 14
5. Buckwheat porridge with coconut oil and strawberries 14
6. Veggie and Feta Omelette 15
7. Cottage Cheese Pancakes with Berry Sauce 15
8. Coconut Pancakes with Maple Butter 16
9. Baked Apples with Walnuts and Cinnamon 16
10. Nutty Granola with Dried Fruits 17
11. Baked Eggs in Avocado 17
12. Veggie Skillet Scramble 18
13. Spinach and Tomato Omelette 18
14. Chia Mango Pudding with Granola 19
15. Tomato and Avocado Toasts 19
16. Mixed Fruit Salad with Mint Yogurt 20
17. Quinoa Veggie Omelette with Cheese 20

Chapter 3. Wholesome Lunch Ideas 21

18. Baked Salmon with Vegetable Couscous 21
19. Turkish Quinoa Salad with Feta 22
20. Chicken Schnitzel with Vegetable Side 22

21. Asparagus with Omelette and Whole Wheat Crackers...................23
22. Cauliflower with Steamed Vegetables and Buckwheat...................23
23. Asian Vegetable Soup with Shrimp...................24
24. Tofu in Soy Sauce with Brown Rice and Broccoli...................24
25. Buckwheat Porridge with Pumpkin Seeds and Sautéed Spinach...................25
26. Roasted Vegetable Salad with Cilantro and Lemon Dressing...................25
27. Couscous with Beef Ragout and Green Peas...................26
28. Stuffed Peppers with Oat Rice and Tomato Sauce...................26
29. Spicy Chicken Chili with Avocado...................27
30. Vegetable Patties with Grated Carrots and Buckwheat Sauce...................27
31. Veal Kebab with Mashed Potatoes and Grilled Vegetables...................28
32. Radish and Apple Salad with Greek Yogurt Dressing...................28
33. Crab Salad with Avocado and Mixed Greens...................29
34. Mushroom Risotto with Parmesan...................29
35. Chicken Patties with Mashed Potatoes and Green Peas...................30
36. Mexican Beef Fajitas with Sautéed Veggies...................30
37. Vegetable Lasagna with Meaty Tomato Sauce...................31

Chapter 4: Dinner Delights 32

38. Grilled Lemon Herb Chicken with Roasted Vegetables...................32
39. Quinoa Stuffed Bell Peppers with Turkey...................33
40. Baked Cod with Tomato and Olive Relish...................33
41. Spinach and Mushroom Frittata with Sweet Potato Hash...................34
42. Zucchini Noodles with Pesto and Cherry Tomatoes...................34
43. Teriyaki Tofu with Broccoli and Jasmine Rice...................35
44. Cauliflower Crust Pizza with Mediterranean Toppings...................35
45. Eggplant Parmesan with Whole Grain Garlic Bread...................36

46. Thai Coconut Curry with Tofu and Vegetables 36

47. Lemon Garlic Salmon with Steamed Asparagus..................................37

48. Beef and Broccoli Stir-Fry with Quinoa 37

49. Ratatouille with Herbed Couscous 38

50. Stuffed Acorn Squash with Wild Rice and Cranberries......................38

51. Chicken Enchilada Casserole with Black Beans and Corn..................39

52. Mushroom Risotto with Peas and Parmesan...................................39

53. Lentil Curry with Cauliflower Rice 40

54. Turkey Meatballs in Marinara Sauce with Whole Wheat Spaghetti........40

55. Sweet and Sour Pork Stir-Fry with Pineapple..................................42

Chapter 5: Nourishing Salads 43

56. Greek Salad with Lemon Herb Dressing..43

57. Caprese Salad with Balsamic Glaze 44

58. Asian Sesame Chicken Salad 44

59. Mango Avocado Salad with Chili Lime Dressing.............................45

60. Cobb Salad with Creamy Avocado Dressing..................................45

61. Roasted Beet and Goat Cheese Salad 46

62. Spinach Strawberry Salad with Poppy Seed Dressing........................46

63. Mediterranean Chickpea Salad with Feta 47

64. Arugula, Pear, and Walnut Salad with Honey Dijon Dressing.............47

65. Shrimp and Mango Quinoa Salad 48

66. Mexican Street Corn Salad 48

67. Watermelon Feta Salad with Mint 49

68. Tuna Nicoise Salad 49

69. Broccoli Crunch Salad with Bacon and Sunflower Seeds....................50

70. Warm Lentil Salad with Roasted Vegetables 50

71. Orzo Pasta Salad with Mediterranean Vegetables 51

72. Apple Walnut Salad with Maple Dijon Vinaigrette 51

73. Thai Beef Salad with Peanut Dressing 52

74. Roasted Cauliflower and Chickpea Salad with Lemon Tahini Dressing. 52

Chapter 6: Plant-Based Cuisine 54

75. Quinoa and Black Bean Salad 54

76. Spicy Tofu Stir-Fry 55

77. Eggplant Parmesan 55

78. Vegan Stuffed Bell Peppers 56

79. Cauliflower Fried Rice 56

80. Black Bean and Sweet Potato Tacos 57

81. Vegan Pad Thai 57

82. Roasted Vegetable Quinoa Bowl 58

83. Zucchini Noodles with Vegan Pesto 58

84. Portobello Mushroom Burgers 59

85. Vegan Creamy Mushroom Risotto 59

86. Chickpea and Vegetable Curry 60

87. Sweet Potato and Chickpea Buddha Bowl 61

Chapter 7. Keto-Friendly Recipes 62

88. Keto Lemon Garlic Butter Salmon 62

89. Cauliflower Crust Pizza with Chicken and Pesto 63

90. Avocado Bacon Egg Cups 63

91. Zucchini Noodles with Creamy Alfredo Sauce 64

92. Keto Chicken and Vegetable Stir-Fry 64

93. Grilled Steak with Garlic Butter 65

94. Coconut Curry Shrimp with Cauliflower Rice 65

95. Bacon-Wrapped Asparagus Bundles 66
96. Eggplant Lasagna with Ricotta and Spinach... 66
97. Turkey Avocado Lettuce Wraps 67
98. Low-Carb Taco Stuffed Peppers.. 67
99. Spinach and Feta Stuffed Chicken Breasts-... 68
100. Keto Beef and Broccoli... 68
101. Creamy Garlic Parmesan Zoodles... 69
102. Mediterranean Grilled Vegetable Salad... 69

Chapter 8. Gluten-Free Delights 70

103. Green Quinoa and Avocado Salad.. 70
104. Gluten-Free Oat Banana Pancakes 71
105. Mushroom Quinoa Patties with Green Peas... 71
106. Sesame Cauliflower with Teriyaki Sauce... 72
107. Caprese Salad with Red Quinoa 72
108. Baked Sweet Potatoes with Walnuts and Cranberries............................. 73
109. Shrimp Coconut Milk Soup 73
110. Thai Shrimp Salad with Sesame Dressing... 74
111. Spinach Avocado Pesto with Gluten-Free Pasta....................................... 74
112. Grilled Turmeric and Ginger Chicken... 75
113. 113Asparagus with Sautéed Mushrooms and Almonds......................... 75
114. Tuna Steak in Teriyaki Sauce with Quinoa.. 76
115. Creamy Broccoli Almond Soup... 76

Chapter 9. Dairy-Free Options 77

116. Vegan Cauliflower Mac and Cheese... 77
117. Almond Milk Smoothie Bowl with Mixed Fruits..................................... 78

118. Dairy-Free Vegetable Curry with Quinoa...78

119. Vegan Coconut Curry Lentil Soup...79

120. Vegan Chickpea Salad Sandwiches...79

121. Cashew Milk Creamy Pasta Primavera..80

122. Vegan Creamy Tomato Basil Soup...80

123. Dairy-Free Pumpkin Coconut Soup...81

124. Vegan Cashew Cheese Stuffed Mushrooms..81

125. Coconut Milk Green Curry Stir-Fry...82

Chapter 10. Healthy Dessert Delights 83

126. Berry Chia Seed Pudding 83

127. Avocado Chocolate Mousse 84

128. Banana Oat Cookies 84

129. Coconut Yogurt Parfait with Fresh Fruit 85

130. Almond Butter Energy Balls 85

131. Baked Apples with Cinnamon and Walnuts..86

132. Mango Coconut Nice Cream...86

133. Chocolate Covered Strawberries...87

134. Quinoa Coconut Macaroons 87

135. Pumpkin Spice Baked Oatmeal Bars 88

136. Raspberry Almond Flour Cake 88

137. Lemon Poppy Seed Muffins with Greek Yogurt Glaze........................89

138. Peach Crisp with Almond Flouropping..89

139. Kiwi Lime Sorbet 90

140. Carrot Cake Energy Bites 90

141. Chocolate Avocado Pudding 91

Chapter 11: Aquatic Delights: Refreshing Recipes..........92
142. Lemon Lime Infused Water..........92
143. Cucumber Mint Detox Water..........93
144. Strawberry Basil Infusion..........93
145. Orange Ginger Splash..........94
146. Blueberry Lavender Elixir..........94
147. Pineapple Coconut Refresher..........95
148. Raspberry Rosemary Infusion..........95
149. Kiwi Strawberry Splash..........96
150. Peach Thyme Hydration..........96
151. Cherry Vanilla Bliss..........97
152. Grapefruit Rose Petal Elixir..........97
153. Mango Pineapple Paradise..........98
154. Blackberry Sage Infused Water..........98
155. Apple Cinnamon Quencher..........99
156. Raspberry Water Infusion..........99

Conclusion..........100

Introduction

Welcome to "The Ultimate Clean Eating Guide: 365 Days of Clean Eating for Weight Loss, Health Support, and Vitality." In this comprehensive guide, you'll discover a year's worth of delicious and nutritious recipes tailored to help you achieve your health and wellness goals. Clean eating isn't just a diet; it's a lifestyle. It's about nourishing your body with whole, minimally processed foods that fuel your energy, support your immune system, and promote overall well-being. Whether you're looking to shed extra pounds, boost your metabolism, or simply adopt a healthier way of eating, this book has you covered.

Inside, you'll find a diverse array of recipes meticulously crafted to tantalize your taste buds while keeping your health in mind. From vibrant salads and hearty soups to satisfying mains and guilt-free desserts, each recipe is designed to showcase the natural flavors and goodness of wholesome ingredients.

But this book is more than just a collection of recipes. It's a guide to transforming your relationship with food and embracing a lifestyle that prioritizes your health and vitality. You'll learn the principles of clean eating, including how to make informed choices at the grocery store, stock your pantry with nutritious staples, and create balanced meals that leave you feeling satisfied and energized.

Whether you're a seasoned clean eater or just starting your journey toward better health, "The Ultimate Clean Eating Guide" is your companion for a year of flavorful, nourishing, and transformative eating. Get ready to revitalize your body, uplift your spirit, and embark on a delicious adventure toward a healthier, happier you.

Chapter 1. The Groundwork: Must-Know Basics

Principles of Clean Eating:

Whole Foods: Focus on consuming whole, minimally processed foods that are as close to their natural state as possible. Choose fresh fruits and vegetables, whole grains, lean proteins, and healthy fats over processed and packaged foods.

Limit Added Sugar: Minimize your intake of added sugars, including those found in sugary beverages, processed snacks, and desserts. Opt for natural sources of sweetness like fruit or small amounts of honey or maple syrup when needed.

Avoid Processed Foods: Steer clear of heavily processed foods that contain artificial additives, preservatives, and unhealthy trans fats. Instead, opt for whole food alternatives that provide essential nutrients without added chemicals.

Choose Healthy Fats: Include sources of healthy fats in your diet such as avocados, nuts, seeds, and olive oil. These fats are essential for supporting brain health, hormone production, and overall well-being.

Emphasize Plant-Based Foods: Fill your plate with a variety of colorful fruits and vegetables to provide essential vitamins, minerals, antioxidants, and fiber. Aim to make half of your plate non-starchy vegetables at each meal.

Moderate Protein Intake: Incorporate lean sources of protein such as poultry, fish, beans, lentils, and tofu into your meals. Protein helps to support muscle growth, repair, and overall satiety.

Hydration: Stay hydrated by drinking plenty of water throughout the day. Herbal teas and infused water are also excellent options to add variety and flavor while staying hydrated.

Portion Control: Be mindful of portion sizes and listen to your body's hunger and fullness cues. Avoid overeating by practicing mindful eating and stopping when you feel satisfied, not stuffed.

Include Plenty of Greens: Make green leafy vegetables a staple in your meals as they are rich in vitamins, minerals, and antioxidants. Incorporate spinach, kale, broccoli, and Swiss chard into salads, soups, smoothies, and stir-fries.

Limit Processed Grains: Choose whole grains like quinoa, brown rice, oats, and barley over refined grains like white bread, white rice, and pasta. Whole grains provide more fiber and nutrients, promoting better digestion and sustained energy levels.

By following these principles of clean eating, you'll nourish your body with nutrient-dense foods, support your overall health and well-being, and cultivate sustainable habits for long-term vitality and success.

Maintaining Hydration Balance:

Proper hydration is essential for overall health and well-being. Here's why it matters and how to ensure you're getting enough water:

1. Body Function: Water is crucial for regulating body temperature, flushing out toxins, and transporting nutrients. It supports physical and mental performance.
2. Preventing Dehydration: Dehydration can lead to fatigue, headaches, and impaired cognitive function. Drink water regularly to avoid it.
3. Water Needs: Aim for at least 8 glasses of water per day, adjusting based on factors like activity level and climate.
4. Listen to Your Body: Drink water throughout the day, especially when you feel thirsty. Thirst is a sign of dehydration.
5. Monitor Urine: Pale yellow urine indicates proper hydration, while dark yellow suggests dehydration.
6. Hydrating Foods: Consume fruits, vegetables, soups, and herbal teas for added hydration.
7. Limit Dehydrating Drinks: Be mindful of alcohol, caffeine, and sugary drinks, which can increase fluid loss.
8. Hydration Tips: Carry a water bottle, set reminders to drink water, and add flavor with fruits or herbs.

Prioritize hydration to support vital functions, improve health, and boost energy levels.

Clean Eating: Quick Guide

Half Plate Rule - Veggies and Greens: Green vegetables are the cornerstone of a healthy diet. Ensure that half of your plate is filled with fresh vegetables and greens at each meal.

Morning Ritual - Water Intake: Upon waking up, drink a glass of warm water with lemon. This helps hydrate the body, cleanse the digestive system, and prepare it for food intake.

Meal with a Gap: Aim to leave about 12-13 hours between dinner and breakfast. This fasting period allows the body to process food, stimulates cell renewal, and enhances overall health.

Sugar Awareness: Minimize your sugar intake by avoiding processed foods and opting for natural sweeteners like honey or maple syrup. Excessive sugar consumption can lead to various health issues, including weight gain and inflammation.

Follow these simple clean eating principles to maintain balance and improve your health.

Chapter 2. Breakfasts to Start Your Day Right.

Welcome to our breakfast oasis! In this chapter, we celebrate the essence of a good morning kickstart. Breakfast is hailed as the day's fuel, igniting energy and setting the tone for your day.

From hearty classics like oatmeal and eggs to lighter fare such as smoothie bowls and yogurt parfaits, our recipes cater to diverse tastes and dietary needs. Quick fixes for busy mornings and indulgent brunch ideas for weekends await you.

. Let's transform your breakfast ritual into a delicious and nourishing experience every day!

1. Berry and Nut Oatmeal Bowl

Yield: 4 servings   Cooking time: 10 min

INGREDIENTS
2 cups rolled oats (160g)

4 cups almond milk (960ml)

2 cups mixed berries (strawberries, blueberries, raspberries) (150g)

4 tablespoons chopped nuts (almonds, walnuts, pecans) (60g)

4 tablespoons honey or maple syrup (optional) (60ml)

Pinch of cinnamon (optional)

Nutritional Information (Per Serving):
Calories : 320 kcal
Proteins: 8g
Fats: 11g
Carbs: 49g

DIRECTIONS
In a medium saucepan, combine the rolled oats and almond milk. Bring the mixture to a gentle boil over medium heat, then reduce the heat and simmer for 5-7 minutes, stirring occasionally, until the oats are cooked and creamy.

Once the oats are cooked, remove from heat and transfer to a serving bowl.

Top the oatmeal with the mixed berries and chopped nuts.

Drizzle with honey or maple syrup if desired, and sprinkle with a pinch of cinnamon for extra flavor.

Serve hot and enjoy your delicious and nutritious berry and nut oatmeal bowl!

2. Avocado Toast with Egg and Tomato

Yield: 4 servings	Cooking time: 10 min

INGREDIENTS

4 slices whole grain bread
2 ripe avocados (about 280g)
4 eggs
1 large tomato, sliced (about 200g)
Salt and pepper to taste
Optional toppings: red pepper flakes, chopped fresh herbs, hot sauce

Nutritional Information (Per Serving):
Calories 280 kcal
Proteins: 12g
Fats: 16g
Carbs: 22g

DIRECTIONS

Toast the slices of whole grain bread until golden brown. While the bread is toasting, slice the avocados in half, remove the pits, and scoop the flesh into a bowl. Mash the avocado with a fork until smooth, then season with salt and pepper to taste. Heat a non-stick skillet over medium heat. Crack the eggs into the skillet and cook to your desired doneness (fried, scrambled, or poached).
Once the eggs are cooked, remove them from the skillet and set aside. Spread a generous amount of mashed avocado onto each slice of toasted bread. Top each avocado toast with a cooked egg and a few slices of tomato.
Season with additional salt and pepper if desired, and garnish with optional toppings such as red pepper flakes, chopped fresh herbs, or hot sauce.
Serve immediately and enjoy your delicious avocado toast with egg and tomato!

3. Green Spinach Banana Smoothie

Yield: 4 servings	Cooking time: 15 min

INGREDIENTS

2 cups fresh spinach leaves (about 60g)
2 ripe bananas, peeled and sliced (about 240g)
1 cup plain Greek yogurt (240g)
1 cup almond milk (240ml)
1 tablespoon honey or maple syrup (15ml)
Optional additions: chia seeds, flaxseeds, protein powder

Nutritional Information (Per Serving):
Calories: 150 kcal
Protein: 6g
Fats: 2g
Carbs: 29g

DIRECTIONS

Place the fresh spinach leaves, sliced bananas, Greek yogurt, almond milk, and honey or maple syrup into a blender. Blend on high speed until the mixture is smooth and creamy, about 1-2 minutes.
If desired, add optional additions such as chia seeds, flaxseeds, or protein powder, and blend again until well combined.
Taste the smoothie and adjust sweetness if necessary by adding more honey or maple syrup.
Pour the green spinach banana smoothie into glasses and serve immediately.

4. Quinoa Fruit Salad with Minty Yogurt

Yield: 4 servings   Cooking time: 20 min

INGREDIENTS

1 cup quinoa, rinsed and cooked (185g cooked)
1 cup mixed fresh fruits (such as berries, mango, pineapple) (150g)
1/4 cup chopped fresh mint leaves (15g)
1/2 cup Greek yogurt (120g)
2 tablespoons honey (30ml)
Juice of 1 lime
Zest of 1 lime
Optional toppings: sliced almonds, shredded coconut

Nutritional Information (Per Serving):
Calories 200 kcal
Proteins: 6 g
Fats: 2g
Carbs: 40g

DIRECTIONS

Cook the quinoa according to package instructions. Once cooked, let it cool to room temperature.

In a large mixing bowl, combine the cooked quinoa and mixed fresh fruits.

In a separate small bowl, mix together the Greek yogurt, honey, chopped fresh mint leaves, lime juice, and lime zest until well combined.

Pour the minty yogurt mixture over the quinoa and fruit mixture. Gently toss until everything is evenly coated.

Divide the salad into individual serving bowls.

Garnish with optional toppings such as sliced almonds or shredded coconut, if desired.

Serve immediately, or refrigerate for 30 minutes to allow flavors to meld before serving.

Enjoy your refreshing and nutritious quinoa fruit salad with minty yogurt!

5. Buckwheat porridge with coconut oil and strawberries

Yield: 4 servings   Cooking time: 15 min

INGREDIENTS

1 cup buckwheat groats (185g)
2 cups water (480ml)
1 cup coconut milk (240ml)
1 tablespoon coconut oil (15ml)
1 teaspoon vanilla extract (5ml)
Pinch of salt
Fresh strawberries, sliced, for serving
Optional toppings: honey, maple syrup, chopped nuts, shredded coconut

Nutritional Information (Per Serving):
Calories: 250 kcal
Protein: 6g
Fats: 10 g
Carbs: 35 g

DIRECTIONS

Rinse the buckwheat groats under cold water.

In a medium saucepan, bring the water to a boil. Add the rinsed buckwheat groats and reduce the heat to low. Simmer for about 10-12 minutes, or until the groats are tender and the water is absorbed.

Stir in the coconut milk, coconut oil, vanilla extract, and a pinch of salt. Cook for an additional 2-3 minutes, stirring occasionally, until the porridge reaches your desired consistency.

Remove the porridge from the heat and let it sit for a few minutes to thicken.

Serve the coconut oil buckwheat porridge warm, topped with fresh sliced strawberries and any optional toppings of your choice.

Enjoy your delicious and nutritious breakfast porridge!

6. Veggie and Feta Omelette

Yield: 4 servings Cooking time: 10 min

INGREDIENTS

6 large eggs
1/4 cup diced bell peppers (about 40g)
1/4 cup diced tomatoes (about 40g)
1/4 cup diced onions (about 40g)
1/4 cup chopped spinach (about 15g)
1/4 cup crumbled feta cheese (about 30g)
Salt and pepper, to taste
1 tablespoon olive oil (15ml)
Fresh herbs (such as parsley or chives) for garnish

Nutritional Information (Per Serving):
Calories 200 kcal
Proteins: 12 g
Fats: 14 g
Carbs: 5 g

DIRECTIONS

In a bowl, whisk together the eggs until well beaten. Season with salt and pepper.
Heat the olive oil in a non-stick skillet over medium heat.
Add the diced bell peppers, tomatoes, and onions to the skillet. Cook for 2-3 minutes, or until softened.
Add the chopped spinach to the skillet and cook for an additional 1-2 minutes, until wilted.
Pour the beaten eggs into the skillet, covering the vegetables evenly.
Sprinkle the crumbled feta cheese over the top of the eggs.
Cook the omelette for 3-4 minutes, or until the edges are set and the bottom is golden brown.
Carefully flip the omelette in half using a spatula, and cook for an additional 1-2 minutes until the eggs are cooked through.
Slide the omelette onto a serving plate and garnish with fresh herbs.
Serve hot, cut into slices, and enjoy your delicious veggie and feta omelette!

7. Cottage Cheese Pancakes with Berry Sauce

Yield: 4 servings Cooking time: 20 min

INGREDIENTS

1 cup cottage cheese (225g)
2 large eggs
1/4 cup all-purpose flour (30g)
1 tablespoon honey or maple syrup (15ml)
1 teaspoon vanilla extract (5ml)
1/4 teaspoon baking powder
Pinch of salt
Butter or oil for frying
Fresh berries for serving
For the Berry Sauce:
1 cup mixed berries (such as strawberries, blueberries, raspberries) (150g)
2 tablespoons honey or maple syrup (30ml)
Juice of 1/2 lemon

Nutritional Information (Per Serving):
Calories: 250 kcal
Protein: 18 g
Fats: 8 g
Carbs: 27 g

DIRECTIONS

In a blender or food processor, combine the cottage cheese, eggs, flour, honey or maple syrup, vanilla extract, baking powder, and a pinch of salt. Blend until smooth.
Heat a non-stick skillet or griddle over medium heat and lightly grease with butter or oil. Pour about 1/4 cup of the pancake batter onto the skillet for each pancake.
Cook for 2-3 minutes, or until bubbles form on the surface of the pancake and the edges begin to set. Flip the pancakes and cook for an additional 1-2 minutes, or until golden brown and cooked through. Repeat with the remaining batter, greasing the skillet as needed.
While the pancakes are cooking, prepare the berry sauce. In a small saucepan, combine the mixed berries, honey or maple syrup, and lemon juice. Cook over medium heat, stirring occasionally, until the berries break down and the sauce thickens slightly, about 5-7 minutes. Remove from heat and set aside. Serve the cottage cheese pancakes warm, topped with the berry sauce and fresh berries.
Enjoy your delicious and nutritious cottage cheese pancakes with berry sauce!

8. Coconut Pancakes with Maple Butter

Yield: 4 servings   Cooking time: 20 min

INGREDIENTS

1 cup all-purpose flour (120g)

1/2 cup shredded coconut (40g)

2 tablespoons sugar (30g)

1 teaspoon baking powder

1/4 teaspoon salt

1 cup coconut milk (240ml)

2 large eggs

2 tablespoons coconut oil, melted (30ml)

1 teaspoon vanilla extract (5ml)

Butter for frying

For the Maple Butter:

4 tablespoons unsalted butter, softened (60g)

2 tablespoons maple syrup (30ml)

Nutritional Information
(Per Serving):
Calories 300 kcal
Proteins: 6 g
Fats: 16 g
Carbs: 34 g

DIRECTIONS

In a large bowl, whisk together the flour, shredded coconut, sugar, baking powder, and salt.

In a separate bowl, whisk together the coconut milk, eggs, melted coconut oil, and vanilla extract.

Pour the wet ingredients into the dry ingredients and stir until just combined. Do not overmix; the batter may be slightly lumpy.

Heat a non-stick skillet or griddle over medium heat and lightly grease with butter.

Pour about 1/4 cup of batter onto the skillet for each pancake. Cook for 2-3 minutes, or until bubbles form on the surface of the pancake and the edges begin to set.

Flip the pancakes and cook for an additional 1-2 minutes, or until golden brown and cooked through.

While the pancakes are cooking, prepare the maple butter. In a small bowl, mix together the softened butter and maple syrup until well combined.

Serve the coconut pancakes warm, topped with a dollop of maple butter.

Enjoy your delicious and fluffy coconut pancakes with maple butter!

9. Baked Apples with Walnuts and Cinnamon

Yield: 4 servings   Cooking time: 40 min

INGREDIENTS

4 large apples (approximately 800g)

1/4 cup chopped walnuts (30g)

2 tablespoons honey or maple syrup (30ml)

1 teaspoon ground cinnamon

1/4 teaspoon ground nutmeg

1 tablespoon unsalted butter, melted (15ml)

1/4 cup water (60ml)

Nutritional Information
(Per Serving):
Calories: 150 kcal
Protein: 1 g
Fats: 5 g
Carbs: 30 g

DIRECTIONS

Preheat your oven to 375°F (190°C).

Wash the apples and core them using an apple corer or a small knife, leaving the bottoms intact.

In a small bowl, mix together the chopped walnuts, honey or maple syrup, ground cinnamon, and ground nutmeg.

Stuff each cored apple with the walnut mixture, dividing it evenly among the apples.

Place the stuffed apples in a baking dish and drizzle with melted butter.

Pour the water into the bottom of the baking dish to prevent the apples from drying out.

Cover the baking dish with aluminum foil and bake in the preheated oven for 20-25 minutes, or until the apples are tender.

Remove the foil and continue baking for an additional 5-10 minutes, or until the tops are golden brown.

Serve the baked apples warm, optionally topped with a dollop of Greek yogurt or a sprinkle of additional cinnamon.

Enjoy your comforting and delicious baked apples with walnuts and cinnamon!

10. Nutty Granola with Dried Fruits

Yield: 8 servings Cooking time: 40 min

INGREDIENTS

1 cup all-purpose flour (120g)
1/2 cup shredded coconut (40g)
2 tablespoons sugar (30g)
1 teaspoon baking powder
1/4 teaspoon salt
1 cup coconut milk (240ml)
2 large eggs
2 tablespoons coconut oil, melted (30ml)
1 teaspoon vanilla extract (5ml)
Butter for frying
For the Maple Butter:
4 tablespoons unsalted butter, softened (60g)
2 tablespoons maple syrup (30ml

Nutritional Information (Per Serving):
Calories 250 kcal
Proteins: 5 g
Fats: 11 g
Carbs: 33 g

DIRECTIONS

Preheat your oven to 325°F (160°C) and line a baking sheet with parchment paper.
In a large mixing bowl, combine the rolled oats, chopped nuts, seeds, shredded coconut, honey or maple syrup, melted coconut oil, vanilla extract, ground cinnamon, and a pinch of salt. Mix well until everything is evenly coated.
Spread the granola mixture in an even layer on the prepared baking sheet.
Bake in the preheated oven for 25-30 minutes, stirring halfway through, or until the granola is golden brown and crisp.
Remove the baking sheet from the oven and let the granola cool completely on the pan.
Once cooled, stir in the dried fruits.
Transfer the nutty granola with dried fruits to an airtight container for storage.
Serve with yogurt, milk, or enjoy it as a snack on its own!
Enjoy your delicious and nutritious nutty granola with dried fruits!

11. Baked Eggs in Avocado

Yield: 4 servings Cooking time: 20 min

INGREDIENTS

2 ripe avocados

4 eggs

Salt and pepper, to taste

Optional toppings: chopped fresh herbs (such as parsley or chives), grated cheese, cooked bacon or sausage

Nutritional Information (Per Serving):
Calories: 150 kcal
Protein: 7 g
Fats: 15 g
Carbs: 9 g

DIRECTIONS

Preheat your oven to 375°F (190°C).
Cut the avocados in half and remove the pits. Scoop out a little extra avocado flesh from each half to make room for the eggs.
Place the avocado halves cut side up on a baking sheet lined with parchment paper.
Crack one egg into each avocado half, making sure the yolks are centered and don't overflow.
Season the eggs with salt and pepper, to taste.
Optional: top each egg with your desired toppings, such as chopped fresh herbs, grated cheese, cooked bacon or sausage.
Bake in the preheated oven for 15-20 minutes, or until the egg whites are set and the yolks reach your desired level of doneness.
Remove from the oven and let cool for a few minutes before serving.
Enjoy your delicious and nutritious baked eggs in avocado!

12. Veggie Skillet Scramble

Yield: 4 servings Cooking time: 15 min

INGREDIENTS

1 tablespoon olive oil (15ml)
1 small onion, diced
1 bell pepper, diced
1 small zucchini, diced (about 150g)
1 cup sliced mushrooms (100g)
2 cups baby spinach (60g)
4 large eggs
Salt and pepper, to taste
Optional toppings: chopped fresh herbs (such as parsley or cilantro), grated cheese, hot sauce

Nutritional Information (Per Serving):
Calories 150 kcal
Proteins: 8 g
Fats: 9 g
Carbs: 10 g

DIRECTIONS

Heat the olive oil in a large skillet over medium heat.
Add the diced onion and bell pepper to the skillet and sauté for 3-4 minutes, or until softened.
Add the diced zucchini and sliced mushrooms to the skillet and continue to cook for another 3-4 minutes, or until the vegetables are tender.
Stir in the baby spinach and cook until wilted, about 1-2 minutes.
In a separate bowl, whisk together the eggs with a pinch of salt and pepper.
Pour the whisked eggs over the cooked vegetables in the skillet.
Gently scramble the eggs with the vegetables until they are cooked through and no longer runny, about 3-4 minutes.
Season the veggie skillet scramble with additional salt and pepper, to taste.
Optional: top with chopped fresh herbs, grated cheese, or hot sauce before serving.
Serve hot and enjoy your delicious and nutritious veggie skillet scramble!

13. Spinach and Tomato Omelette

Yield: 2 servings Cooking time: 10 min

INGREDIENTS

2 ripe avocados
4 eggs
Salt and pepper, to taste
Optional toppings: chopped fresh herbs (such as parsley or chives), grated cheese, cooked bacon or sausage

Nutritional Information (Per Serving):
Calories: 200 kcal
Protein: 12 g
Fats: 15 g
Carbs: 4 g

DIRECTIONS

In a bowl, beat the eggs with a pinch of salt and pepper until well combined. Heat the olive oil in a non-stick skillet over medium heat. Add the spinach leaves to the skillet and cook for 1-2 minutes, or until wilted.
Add the diced tomato to the skillet and cook for another 1-2 minutes, until softened.
Spread the spinach and tomato evenly in the skillet and pour the beaten eggs over the vegetables.
Cook the omelette for 3-4 minutes, or until the edges start to set.
Using a spatula, gently lift the edges of the omelette and tilt the skillet to allow the uncooked eggs to flow to the bottom.
Continue cooking until the omelette is set but still slightly runny on top.
Optional: sprinkle grated cheese over one half of the omelette and fold the other half over the top.
Slide the omelette onto a plate, sprinkle with chopped fresh herbs if desired, and serve hot.
Enjoy your delicious and nutritious spinach and tomato omelette!

14. Chia Mango Pudding with Granola

Yield: 2 servings Cooking time: 10 min

INGREDIENTS

- 1 ripe mango, peeled and diced (about 200g)
- 1/2 cup unsweetened almond milk (120ml)
- 2 tablespoons chia seeds (30g)
- 1/2 teaspoon vanilla extract (2.5ml)
- 1/4 cup granola (30g)
- Optional toppings: sliced mango, shredded coconut, chopped nuts

DIRECTIONS

In a blender or food processor, purée the diced mango until smooth.

In a mixing bowl, combine the mango purée, almond milk, chia seeds, and vanilla extract. Stir well to combine.

Cover the bowl and refrigerate the mixture for at least 2 hours, or until it thickens into a pudding-like consistency. You can also leave it overnight for best results.

Once the chia pudding has set, divide it between two serving glasses or bowls.

Top each serving with granola and any optional toppings of your choice, such as sliced mango, shredded coconut, or chopped nuts.

Serve chilled and enjoy your delicious and nutritious chia mango pudding with granola!

Nutritional Information (Per Serving):
Calories 250 kcal
Proteins: 5 g
Fats: 8 g
Carbs: 40 g

15. Tomato and Avocado Toasts

Yield: 2 servings Cooking time: 10 min

INGREDIENTS

- 2 ripe avocados
- 4 eggs
- Salt and pepper, to taste
- Optional toppings: chopped fresh herbs (such as parsley or chives), grated cheese, cooked bacon or sausage

DIRECTIONS

Toast the slices of whole grain bread until golden brown and crispy.

While the bread is toasting, halve the avocado and remove the pit. Scoop the avocado flesh into a small bowl and mash it with a fork until smooth.

Season the mashed avocado with salt and pepper, to taste.

Once the toast is ready, spread the mashed avocado evenly over each slice.

Arrange the thinly sliced tomato on top of the avocado spread.

Season the tomato slices with a little more salt and pepper, if desired.

Optional: garnish the toasts with red pepper flakes, a drizzle of balsamic glaze, or fresh basil leaves for extra flavor.

Serve immediately and enjoy your delicious and nutritious tomato and avocado toasts!

Nutritional Information (Per Serving):
Calories: 200 kcal
Protein: 4 g
Fats: 10 g
Carbs: 24 g

16. Mixed Fruit Salad with Mint Yogurt

Yield: 4 servings   Cooking time: 15 min

INGREDIENTS

2 cups mixed fresh fruits (such as berries, grapes, pineapple, mango, kiwi) (about 300g)
1/2 cup plain Greek yogurt (120g)
1 tablespoon honey (15ml)
1 tablespoon fresh mint leaves, finely chopped
Optional toppings: toasted coconut flakes, chopped nuts, granola

DIRECTIONS

Wash and prepare the mixed fresh fruits as needed. Cut larger fruits into bite-sized pieces.
In a small bowl, mix together the Greek yogurt, honey, and finely chopped mint leaves until well combined.
Arrange the mixed fresh fruits in a serving bowl or on a platter.
Drizzle the mint yogurt dressing over the fruits or serve it on the side as a dipping sauce.
Optional: sprinkle toasted coconut flakes, chopped nuts, or granola over the fruit salad for added texture and flavor.
Serve immediately and enjoy your refreshing and nutritious mixed fruit salad with mint yogurt!

Nutritional Information (Per Serving):
Calories 120 kcal
Proteins: 3 g
Fats: 0 g
Carbs: 25 g

17. Quinoa Veggie Omelette with Cheese

Yield: 2 servings   Cooking time: 15 min

INGREDIENTS

4 large eggs
1/2 cup cooked quinoa (90g)
1/2 cup mixed diced vegetables (such as bell peppers, onions, mushrooms) (about 80g)
1/4 cup shredded cheese (such as cheddar or mozzarella) (about 30g)
1 tablespoon olive oil (15ml)
Salt and pepper, to taste
Optional toppings: salsa, avocado slices, fresh herbs

DIRECTIONS

In a bowl, beat the eggs with a pinch of salt and pepper until well combined. Heat the olive oil in a non-stick skillet over medium heat. Add the mixed diced vegetables to the skillet and sauté for 3-4 minutes, or until softened.
Stir in the cooked quinoa and cook for another 2 minutes, stirring occasionally.
Pour the beaten eggs over the quinoa and vegetable mixture in the skillet. Allow the eggs to cook undisturbed for a few minutes until the edges start to set. Sprinkle the shredded cheese evenly over one half of the omelette.
Using a spatula, gently fold the other half of the omelette over the cheese-covered half.
Continue cooking for another 2-3 minutes, or until the cheese is melted and the eggs are cooked through.
Slide the omelette onto a plate, cut it in half, and serve immediately.
Optional: garnish with salsa, avocado slices, or fresh herbs before serving.
Enjoy your delicious and nutritious quinoa veggie omelette with cheese!

Nutritional Information (Per Serving):
Calories: 300 kcal
Protein: 18 g
Fats: 18 g
Carbs: 15 g

Chapter 2. Wholesome Lunch Ideas.

Welcome to the chapter on wholesome lunch ideas! Here, you'll discover a variety of nutritious and delicious recipes perfect for fueling your midday break. From vibrant salads to hearty soups and satisfying sandwiches, these recipes are designed to keep you energized and satisfied throughout the day. Whether you're at home, work, or on the go, these dishes will nourish your body and delight your taste buds. So, let's dive in and explore these wholesome lunch options!

18. Baked Salmon with Vegetable Couscous

Yield: 4 servings   Cooking time: 30 min

INGREDIENTS

4 salmon fillets (about 6 ounces each) (680g)
1 cup couscous (185g)
1 ½ cups vegetable broth (360ml)
1 tablespoon olive oil (15ml)
1 small onion, finely chopped
2 cloves garlic, minced
1 bell pepper, diced (about 150g)
1 zucchini, diced (about 150g)
1 carrot, diced (about 75g)
Salt and pepper to taste
Fresh herbs for garnish (optional)

Nutritional Information
(Per Serving):
Calories : 350 kcal
Proteins: 25 g
Fats: 12 g
Carbs: 30 g

DIRECTIONS

Preheat the oven to 375°F (190°C).
Season the salmon fillets with salt and pepper, then place them on a baking sheet lined with parchment paper.
Bake the salmon in the preheated oven for 12-15 minutes, or until cooked through and flakes easily with a fork.
While the salmon is baking, prepare the vegetable couscous. In a medium saucepan, heat the olive oil over medium heat. Add the chopped onion and garlic to the saucepan and cook until softened and fragrant, about 2-3 minutes. Stir in the diced bell pepper, zucchini, and carrot. Cook for another 5 minutes, or until the vegetables are tender. Pour in the vegetable broth and bring to a boil. Once boiling, stir in the couscous, cover the saucepan, and remove from heat. Let it sit for 5 minutes to allow the couscous to absorb the broth.
Fluff the couscous with a fork and season with salt and pepper to taste.
Serve the baked salmon fillets with a generous portion of vegetable couscous.
Garnish with fresh herbs if desired.
Enjoy your delicious and nutritious baked salmon with vegetable couscous!

19. Turkish Quinoa Salad with Feta

Yield: 4 servings Cooking time: 45 min

INGREDIENTS

1 cup quinoa, rinsed (185g)
2 cups water (480ml)
1 cucumber, diced (about 200g)
1 bell pepper, diced (about 150g)
1 tomato, diced (about 150g)
1/2 red onion, finely chopped (about 50g)
1/4 cup fresh parsley, chopped (15g)
1/4 cup fresh mint leaves, chopped (15g)
1/2 cup crumbled feta cheese (about 100g)
Juice of 1 lemon
2 tablespoons olive oil (30ml)
Salt and pepper to taste

Nutritional Information (Per Serving):
Calories 280 kcal
Proteins: 9 g
Fats: 12 g
Carbs: 33 g

DIRECTIONS

In a medium saucepan, bring the water to a boil. Add the quinoa, reduce heat to low, cover, and simmer for 15 minutes, or until the quinoa is cooked and water is absorbed. Remove from heat and let it cool.
In a large mixing bowl, combine the cooked quinoa, diced cucumber, bell pepper, tomato, red onion, chopped parsley, and chopped mint leaves.
In a small bowl, whisk together the lemon juice and olive oil.
Pour the dressing over the salad and toss to combine.
Gently fold in the crumbled feta cheese.
Season with salt and pepper to taste.
Serve the Turkish quinoa salad immediately, or refrigerate for at least 30 minutes to allow the flavors to meld.
Enjoy your flavorful and nutritious Turkish quinoa salad with feta!

20. Chicken Schnitzel with Vegetable Side

Yield: 4 servings Cooking time: 35 min

INGREDIENTS

4 boneless, skinless chicken breasts (500g)
1/2 cup all-purpose flour (60g)
2 eggs, beaten
1 cup breadcrumbs (about 60g)
2 tablespoons grated Parmesan cheese (15g)
1 teaspoon paprika
Salt and pepper to taste
2 tablespoons olive oil (30ml)
1 tablespoon butter (15g)
1 lemon, cut into wedges
For the Vegetable Side:
2 cups mixed vegetables (such as carrots, green beans, and bell peppers), chopped (about 300g)
2 cloves garlic, minced
2 tablespoons olive oil (30ml)
Salt and pepper to taste

Nutritional Information (Per Serving):
Calories: 300 kcal
Protein: 30 g
Fats: 15 g
Carbs: 20 g

DIRECTIONS

Preheat the oven to 200°C (400°F). Place the chicken breasts between two sheets of plastic wrap and pound them to an even thickness using a meat mallet or rolling pin. Set up three shallow bowls: one with flour, one with beaten eggs, and one with breadcrumbs mixed with Parmesan cheese, paprika, salt, and pepper. Dredge each chicken breast in the flour, then dip it into the beaten eggs, and finally coat it with the breadcrumb mixture, pressing gently to adhere. Heat the olive oil and butter in a large ovenproof skillet over medium heat. Add the breaded chicken breasts to the skillet and cook for 3-4 minutes on each side, or until golden brown. Transfer the skillet to the preheated oven and bake for 8-10 minutes, or until the chicken is cooked through and reaches an internal temperature of 75°C (165°F). While the chicken is baking, prepare the vegetable side. In a separate skillet, heat the olive oil over medium heat. Add the minced garlic and sauté for 1 minute, until fragrant. Add the chopped mixed vegetables to the skillet and cook for 5-7 minutes, or until tender-crisp. Season with salt and pepper to taste. Serve the chicken schnitzel with the vegetable side and lemon wedges on the side.
Enjoy your delicious and satisfying chicken schnitzel with a flavorful vegetable side!

21. Asparagus with Omelette and Whole Wheat Crackers

Yield: 2 servings   Cooking time: 20 min

INGREDIENTS

1 bunch asparagus, trimmed (about 250g)
4 large eggs
2 tablespoons milk (30ml)
Salt and pepper to taste
1 tablespoon olive oil (15ml)
4 whole wheat crackers

Nutritional Information (Per Serving):
Calories 250 kcal
Proteins: 15 g
Fats: 15 g
Carbs: 15 g

DIRECTIONS

Heat a large skillet over medium heat and add the olive oil. Add the trimmed asparagus to the skillet and cook for 5-7 minutes, or until tender-crisp, stirring occasionally. Season with salt and pepper to taste. While the asparagus is cooking, crack the eggs into a mixing bowl. Add the milk, salt, and pepper, and whisk until well combined. Pour the egg mixture over the cooked asparagus in the skillet. Cook for 3-4 minutes, or until the eggs are set around the edges. Using a spatula, gently lift the edges of the omelette and tilt the skillet to allow the uncooked eggs to flow underneath. Once the omelette is set but still slightly runny on top, carefully flip it over and cook for another 1-2 minutes. Slide the omelette onto a plate and cut it into wedges. Serve the asparagus and omelette with whole wheat crackers on the side. Enjoy your nutritious and satisfying meal of asparagus with omelette and whole wheat crackers!

22. Cauliflower with Steamed Vegetables and Buckwheat

Yield: 2 servings   Cooking time: 30 min

INGREDIENTS

1 cup buckwheat groats (185g)
2 cups water (480ml)
1 small head cauliflower, cut into florets (about 400g)
1 carrot, sliced (about 100g)
1 zucchini, sliced (about 150g)
1 cup broccoli florets (about 100g)
2 tablespoons olive oil (30ml)
2 cloves garlic, minced
Salt and pepper to taste
Fresh herbs for garnish (optional

Nutritional Information (Per Serving):
Calories: 300 kcal
Protein: 9 g
Fats: 9 g
Carbs: 50 g

DIRECTIONS

Rinse the buckwheat groats under cold water and drain. In a medium saucepan, bring the water to a boil. Add the buckwheat groats, reduce the heat to low, cover, and simmer for 15-20 minutes, or until the buckwheat is tender and the water is absorbed. Remove from heat and let it sit, covered, for 5 minutes.
While the buckwheat is cooking, prepare the steamed vegetables. Place a steamer basket in a pot filled with about 1 inch of water. Bring the water to a boil.
Add the cauliflower florets, sliced carrot, sliced zucchini, and broccoli florets to the steamer basket. Cover and steam for 5-7 minutes, or until the vegetables are tender-crisp.
In a large skillet, heat the olive oil over medium heat. Add the minced garlic and cook for 1-2 minutes, until fragrant. Add the steamed vegetables to the skillet with the garlic and toss to coat. Season with salt and pepper to taste.
Serve the steamed vegetables alongside the cooked buckwheat groats.
Garnish with fresh herbs if desired.
Enjoy your healthy and delicious cauliflower with steamed vegetables and buckwheat!

23. Asian Vegetable Soup with Shrimp

Yield: 4 servings   Cooking time: 25 min

INGREDIENTS

8 cups low-sodium chicken or vegetable broth (1920ml)
1 cup shiitake mushrooms, sliced (about 100g)
1 cup bok choy, chopped (about 150g)
1 cup snow peas, trimmed (about 100g)
1 carrot, julienned (about 100g)
1 red bell pepper, thinly sliced (about 150g)
1 tablespoon fresh ginger, grated
2 cloves garlic, minced
1 tablespoon low-sodium soy sauce (15ml)
1 tablespoon rice vinegar (15ml)
1 teaspoon sesame oil (5ml)
12 ounces raw shrimp, peeled and deveined (about 340g)
Salt and pepper to taste
Thinly sliced green onions and cilantro for garnish

Nutritional Information (Per Serving):
Calories 200 kcal
Proteins: 25 g
Fats: 3 g
Carbs: 15 g

DIRECTIONS

In a large pot, bring the chicken or vegetable broth to a simmer over medium heat.

Add the sliced shiitake mushrooms, chopped bok choy, snow peas, julienned carrot, and thinly sliced red bell pepper to the pot. Cook for 5-7 minutes, or until the vegetables are tender.

Stir in the grated ginger, minced garlic, soy sauce, rice vinegar, and sesame oil. Cook for another 2-3 minutes to allow the flavors to meld.

Add the raw shrimp to the pot and cook for 2-3 minutes, or until the shrimp are pink and opaque.

Season the soup with salt and pepper to taste.

Ladle the Asian vegetable soup into bowls and garnish with thinly sliced green onions and cilantro.

Serve hot and enjoy your light and flavorful Asian vegetable soup with shrimp!

24. Tofu in Soy Sauce with Brown Rice and Broccoli

Yield: 4 servings   Cooking time: 30 min

INGREDIENTS

1 block (14 ounces) firm tofu, pressed and cubed (about 400g)

2 tablespoons low-sodium soy sauce (30ml)

1 tablespoon sesame oil (15ml)

2 cloves garlic, minced

1 tablespoon grated ginger

4 cups cooked brown rice (about 720g)

4 cups broccoli florets (about 400g)

2 tablespoons olive oil (30ml)

Salt and pepper to taste

Sesame seeds for garnish

Nutritional Information (Per Serving):
Calories: 300 kcal
Protein: 15 g
Fats: 12 g
Carbs: 35 g

DIRECTIONS

Preheat the oven to 400°F (200°C).
In a bowl, toss the cubed tofu with the low-sodium soy sauce, sesame oil, minced garlic, and grated ginger until evenly coated.
Arrange the marinated tofu cubes on a baking sheet lined with parchment paper. Bake in the preheated oven for 20-25 minutes, or until golden and crispy.
While the tofu is baking, steam the broccoli florets until tender-crisp, about 5-7 minutes. Set aside.
In a large skillet, heat the olive oil over medium heat. Add the cooked brown rice to the skillet and stir-fry for 2-3 minutes, or until heated through.
Add the steamed broccoli to the skillet with the brown rice and toss to combine. Season with salt and pepper to taste.
Serve the tofu in soy sauce alongside the brown rice and broccoli mixture.
Garnish with sesame seeds.
Enjoy your nutritious and satisfying tofu in soy sauce with brown rice and broccoli!

25. Buckwheat Porridge with Pumpkin Seeds and Sautéed Spinach

Yield: 2 servings Cooking time: 25 min

INGREDIENTS

1/2 cup buckwheat groats (90g)
1 cup water (240ml)
2 cups fresh spinach leaves (about 60g)
2 tablespoons pumpkin seeds (30g)
1 tablespoon olive oil (15ml)
1/2 teaspoon garlic powder
Salt and pepper to taste

Nutritional Information
(Per Serving):
Calories 300 kcal
Proteins: 10 g
Fats: 8 g
Carbs: 50 g

DIRECTIONS

Rinse the buckwheat groats under cold water and drain.

In a small saucepan, bring the water to a boil. Add the rinsed buckwheat groats, reduce the heat to low, cover, and simmer for 15-20 minutes, or until the buckwheat is tender and the water is absorbed. Remove from heat and let it sit, covered, for 5 minutes.

While the buckwheat is cooking, heat the olive oil in a skillet over medium heat. Add the fresh spinach leaves and sauté for 2-3 minutes, or until wilted. Season with garlic powder, salt, and pepper to taste.

Divide the cooked buckwheat porridge between two bowls. Top each bowl of buckwheat porridge with sautéed spinach and pumpkin seeds.

Serve hot and enjoy your wholesome and nutritious buckwheat porridge with pumpkin seeds and sautéed spinach!

26. Roasted Vegetable Salad with Cilantro and Lemon Dressing

Yield: 4 servings Cooking time: 40 min

INGREDIENTS

2 cups mixed vegetables (such as bell peppers, zucchini, cherry tomatoes, and red onion), chopped (about 300g)
2 tablespoons olive oil (30ml)
Salt and pepper to taste
4 cups mixed salad greens (about 120g)
1/4 cup fresh cilantro leaves, chopped (15g)
1 lemon, juiced
2 tablespoons extra-virgin olive oil (30ml)
1 tablespoon honey or maple syrup (15ml)
1 teaspoon Dijon mustard (5ml)

Nutritional Information
(Per Serving):
Calories: 180 kcal
Protein: 2g
Fats: 14 g
Carbs: 14 g

DIRECTIONS

Preheat the oven to 400°F (200°C).
In a large mixing bowl, toss the chopped mixed vegetables with olive oil, salt, and pepper until evenly coated.
Spread the seasoned vegetables in a single layer on a baking sheet lined with parchment paper. Roast the vegetables in the preheated oven for 20-25 minutes, or until they are tender and lightly browned, stirring halfway through the cooking time. While the vegetables are roasting, prepare the salad dressing. In a small bowl, whisk together the lemon juice, extra-virgin olive oil, honey or maple syrup, and Dijon mustard until well combined. In a large salad bowl, combine the mixed salad greens and chopped cilantro. Once the roasted vegetables are done, remove them from the oven and let them cool slightly.
Add the roasted vegetables to the salad bowl with the mixed greens and cilantro.
Drizzle the salad dressing over the salad and toss gently to coat all the ingredients.
Serve immediately and enjoy your flavorful and nutritious roasted vegetable salad with cilantro and lemon dressing!

27. Couscous with Beef Ragout and Green Peas

Yield: 4 servings   Cooking time: 40 min

INGREDIENTS

1 cup couscous (180g)
1 1/2 cups water (360ml)
1 tablespoon olive oil (15ml)
1 onion, diced
2 cloves garlic, minced
1 pound lean beef stew meat, diced (450g)
1 can (14 ounces) diced tomatoes (about 400g)
1 cup beef broth (240ml)
1 teaspoon dried oregano
1 teaspoon dried basil
Salt and pepper to taste
1 cup frozen green peas (about 150g)
Fresh parsley for garnish

Nutritional Information
(Per Serving):
Calories 250 kcal
Proteins: 10 g
Fats: 8 g
Carbs: 50 g

DIRECTIONS

In a medium saucepan, bring the water to a boil. Stir in the couscous, cover, and remove from heat. Let it stand for 5 minutes, then fluff with a fork. In a large skillet, heat the olive oil over medium heat. Add the diced onion and minced garlic, and sauté until softened and fragrant, about 2-3 minutes. Add the diced beef stew meat to the skillet and cook until browned on all sides, about 5 minutes. Stir in the diced tomatoes, beef broth, dried oregano, and dried basil. Season with salt and pepper to taste. Bring the mixture to a simmer, then reduce the heat to low. Cover and let it simmer for 15-20 minutes, or until the beef is tender and the sauce has thickened. Stir in the frozen green peas and cook for an additional 3-5 minutes, or until the peas are heated through. To serve, fluff the cooked couscous with a fork and divide it among serving plates. Top with the beef ragout and green peas mixture. Garnish with fresh parsley. Enjoy your hearty and flavorful couscous with beef ragout and green peas!

28. Stuffed Peppers with Oat Rice and Tomato Sauce

Yield: 4 servings   Cooking time: 60 min

INGREDIENTS

4 large bell peppers, any color
1 cup rolled oats (90g)
2 cups water (480ml)
1 tablespoon olive oil (15ml)
1 onion, diced
2 cloves garlic, minced
1 carrot, grated
1 zucchini, grated
1 cup canned diced tomatoes (about 240g)
1 teaspoon dried oregano
1 teaspoon dried basil
Salt and pepper to taste
Fresh parsley for garnish

Nutritional Information
(Per Serving):
Calories: 250 kcal
Protein: 6 g
Fats: 6 g
Carbs: 45 g

DIRECTIONS

Preheat the oven to 375°F (190°C) and prepare bell peppers by cutting off the tops and removing seeds. Cook rolled oats in boiling water for 10-12 minutes until tender, then set aside. In a skillet, sauté onion and garlic until soft. Add grated carrot, zucchini, canned diced tomatoes, dried herbs, salt, and pepper. Cook for 5 minutes. Combine cooked oats with vegetable mixture and stuff peppers. Place stuffed peppers in a baking dish with a little water at the bottom to prevent drying. Cover with foil and bake for 30-35 minutes until peppers are tender. Remove foil and bake for 5 more minutes until lightly browned. Garnish with parsley and serve hot. Enjoy!

29. Spicy Chicken Chili with Avocado

Yield: 4 servings   Cooking time: 45 min

INGREDIENTS

1 tablespoon olive oil (15ml)
1 onion, diced
2 cloves garlic, minced
450g boneless, skinless chicken breasts, diced
1 can diced tomatoes (about 400g)
1 can black beans, drained and rinsed (400g)
1 can kidney beans, drained and rinsed (400g)
1 cup frozen corn kernels (about 150g)
1 tablespoon chili powder
1 teaspoon ground cumin
1/2 teaspoon paprika
1/4 teaspoon cayenne pepper (adjust to taste)
Salt and pepper to taste
2 cups low-sodium chicken broth (480ml)
1 avocado, diced
Fresh cilantro for garnish
Lime wedges for serving

Nutritional Information (Per Serving):
Calories 250 kcal
Proteins: 10 g
Fats: 8 g
Carbs: 50 g

DIRECTIONS

In a large pot or Dutch oven, heat the olive oil over medium heat. Add the diced onion and minced garlic, and sauté until softened and fragrant, about 2-3 minutes. Add the diced chicken breasts to the pot and cook until browned on all sides, about 5 minutes. Stir in the diced tomatoes (with their juices), black beans, kidney beans, frozen corn kernels, chili powder, ground cumin, paprika, cayenne pepper, salt, and pepper. Pour in the chicken broth and stir to combine.

Bring the chili to a simmer, then reduce the heat to low. Cover and let it simmer for 20-25 minutes, stirring occasionally, until the flavors are well combined and the chili has thickened. Taste and adjust the seasoning if necessary.

To serve, ladle the spicy chicken chili into bowls. Top each bowl with diced avocado and fresh cilantro.

Serve hot with lime wedges on the side.

Enjoy your hearty and flavorful spicy chicken chili with avocado!

30. Vegetable Patties with Grated Carrots and Buckwheat Sauce

Yield: 4 servings   Cooking time: 45 min

INGREDIENTS

1 cup buckwheat groats, cooked (185g)
about 2 medium carrots (120g)
1/2 cup breadcrumbs (60g)
1 small onion chopped (40g)
2 cloves garlic, minced
1/4 cup chopped fresh parsley (about 15g)
1 teaspoon ground cumin
1/2 teaspoon paprika
Salt and pepper to taste
2 tablespoons olive oil (30ml), divided
For the Buckwheat Sauce:
1/2 cup buckwheat groats, cooked (90g)
1 cup vegetable broth (240ml)
1 tablespoon olive oil (15ml)
1 tablespoon lemon juice (15ml)
Salt and pepper to taste

Nutritional Information (Per Serving):
Calories: 280 kcal
Protein: 6 g
Fats: 10 g
Carbs: 40 g

DIRECTIONS

In a large bowl, mix cooked buckwheat, grated carrots, breadcrumbs, onion, garlic, parsley, cumin, paprika, salt, and pepper. Form mixture into patties. Heat olive oil in a skillet over medium heat. Cook patties for 3-4 minutes on each side until golden and crispy. For the buckwheat sauce, simmer buckwheat and vegetable broth for 5-7 minutes until tender. Remove from heat and stir in olive oil, lemon juice, salt, and pepper. Serve patties with buckwheat sauce drizzled on top. Enjoy!

31. Veal Kebab with Mashed Potatoes and Grilled Vegetables

Yield: 4 servings   Cooking time: 45 min

INGREDIENTS

For the Veal Kebab:
1 pound veal meat, diced (about 450g)
1 onion, finely chopped
2 cloves garlic, minced
2 tablespoons olive oil (30ml)
1 teaspoon ground cumin
1 teaspoon paprika
1/2 teaspoon ground coriander
Salt and pepper to taste
Wooden skewers, soaked in water for 30 minutes
For the Mashed Potatoes:
4 medium potatoes, peeled and diced (about 600g)
1/4 cup milk (60ml)
2 tablespoons unsalted butter (30g)
Salt and pepper to taste
For the Grilled Vegetables:
2 bell peppers, sliced
1 zucchini, sliced
1 eggplant, sliced
2 tablespoons olive oil (30ml)
Salt and pepper to taste

Nutritional Information (Per Serving):
Calories: 250 kcal
Proteins: 10 g
Fats: 8 g
Carbs: 50 g

DIRECTIONS

Combine diced veal, onion, garlic, olive oil, cumin, paprika, coriander, salt, and pepper in a bowl.

Thread seasoned veal onto soaked skewers.

Grill kebabs for 8-10 minutes until cooked through and charred. For the Mashed Potatoes:

Boil diced potatoes until tender, then drain.

Return potatoes to the pot and mash with milk and butter until creamy.

Season with salt and pepper. For the Grilled Vegetables:

Toss sliced bell peppers, zucchini, and eggplant with olive oil, salt, and pepper.

Grill for 4-5 minutes on each side until tender and charred.

To Serve:

Arrange veal kebabs on a platter with mashed potatoes and grilled vegetables.

Garnish with fresh herbs if desired.

Serve hot. Enjoy!

32. Radish and Apple Salad with Greek Yogurt Dressing

Yield: 4 servings   Cooking time: 15 min

INGREDIENTS

For the Salad:

200g lump crab meat

2 ripe avocados, diced

4 cups mixed greens (about 120g)

1/4 cup cherry tomatoes, halved (about 50g)

1/4 cup cucumber, sliced (about 50g)

1/4 cup red onion, thinly sliced (about 40g)

For the Dressing:

2 tablespoons extra virgin olive oil (30ml)

1 tablespoon lemon juice (15ml)

1 teaspoon Dijon mustard (5ml)

Salt and pepper to taste

Nutritional Information (Per Serving):
Calories: 150 kcal
Protein: 5 g
Fats: 7 g
Carbs: 18 g

DIRECTIONS

In a large salad bowl, combine the sliced radishes, apple, chopped walnuts, mixed greens, and chopped parsley.

In a separate small bowl, whisk together the Greek yogurt, lemon juice, honey, Dijon mustard, salt, and pepper until well combined.

Pour the Greek yogurt dressing over the salad and toss gently to coat all the ingredients evenly.

Serve immediately as a refreshing and nutritious side dish or light meal.

33. Crab Salad with Avocado and Mixed Greens

Yield: 4 servings   Cooking time: 15 min

INGREDIENTS

For the Salad:
200g lump crab meat
2 ripe avocados, diced
4 cups mixed greens (about 120g)
1/4 cup cherry tomatoes, halved (about 50g)
1/4 cup cucumber, sliced (about 50g)
1/4 cup red onion, thinly sliced (about 40g)
For the Dressing:
2 tablespoons extra virgin olive oil (30ml)
1 tablespoon lemon juice (15ml)
1 teaspoon Dijon mustard (5ml)
Salt and pepper to taste

Nutritional Information (Per Serving):
Calories 220 kcal
Proteins: 10 g
Fats: 15 g
Carbs: 10 g

DIRECTIONS

In a large salad bowl, combine the lump crab meat, diced avocado, mixed greens, cherry tomatoes, sliced cucumber, and thinly sliced red onion.

In a small bowl, whisk together the extra virgin olive oil, lemon juice, Dijon mustard, salt, and pepper to make the dressing.

Drizzle the dressing over the salad and toss gently to coat all the ingredients evenly.

Serve immediately as a light and flavorful salad.

34. Mushroom Risotto with Parmesan

Yield: 4 servings   Cooking time: 60 min

INGREDIENTS

1 cup Arborio rice (200g)
4 cups vegetable broth (960ml)
2 tablespoons olive oil (30ml)
1 onion, finely chopped
2 cloves garlic, minced
200g mushrooms, sliced
1/4 cup dry white wine (60ml)
1/4 cup grated Parmesan cheese (30g)
Salt and pepper to taste
Fresh parsley, chopped, for garnish

Nutritional Information (Per Serving):
Calories: 320 kcal
Protein: 8 g
Fats: 8 g
Carbs: 50 g

DIRECTIONS

Heat vegetable broth in a saucepan over low heat. In a large skillet, sauté chopped onion and minced garlic in olive oil until soft and translucent, about 5 minutes.

Add sliced mushrooms to the skillet and cook until golden brown and tender, about 5-7 minutes. Stir in Arborio rice and cook for another 2 minutes, stirring constantly until rice is coated with oil and slightly translucent.

Pour in dry white wine and cook until evaporated, stirring frequently. Begin adding warm vegetable broth, one ladleful at a time, stirring constantly and allowing each addition to be absorbed before adding more. Continue until the rice is creamy and cooked al dente, about 20-25 minutes.

Once the risotto reaches desired consistency, remove from heat and stir in grated Parmesan cheese until melted and well combined. Season with salt and pepper to taste.

Serve hot, garnished with chopped fresh parsley. Enjoy!

35. Chicken Patties with Mashed Potatoes and Green Peas

Yield: 4 servings   Cooking time: 40 min

INGREDIENTS

For the Chicken Patties:
500g ground chicken
1/4 cup breadcrumbs (30g)
1 egg
1/4 cup grated Parmesan cheese (30g)
1/4 cup chopped fresh parsley (15g)
2 cloves garlic, minced
Salt and pepper to taste
2 tablespoons olive oil (30ml)
For the Mashed Potatoes:
600g medium potatoes, peeled and diced
60ml milk
30g unsalted butter
Salt and pepper to taste
For the Green Peas:
2 cups frozen green peas (about 300g)
30g unsalted butter
Salt and pepper to taste

Nutritional Information
(Per Serving):
Calories 220 kcal
Proteins: 10 g
Fats: 15 g
Carbs: 10 g

DIRECTIONS

Prepare Chicken Patties:
Combine ground chicken, breadcrumbs, egg, Parmesan, parsley, garlic, salt, and pepper.
Shape into patties and cook in olive oil until golden and cooked through (4-5 minutes per side).
Make Mashed Potatoes:
Boil potatoes until tender (15-20 minutes), then mash with milk, butter, salt, and pepper.
Prepare Green Peas:
Cook frozen green peas in melted butter until heated through (5-7 minutes).
Serve:
Plate chicken patties with mashed potatoes and green peas.
Garnish with parsley if desired.
Serve hot.

36. Mexican Beef Fajitas with Sautéed Veggies

Yield: 4 servings   Cooking time: 20 min

INGREDIENTS

1 lb (450g) beef sirloin, thinly sliced
2 bell peppers, thinly sliced
1 onion, thinly sliced
2 tablespoons olive oil
2 cloves garlic, minced
1 teaspoon chili powder
1 teaspoon ground cumin
1 teaspoon paprika
Salt and pepper to taste
Juice of 1 lime
8 small flour tortillas
Optional toppings: salsa, guacamole, sour cream, shredded cheese

Nutritional Information
(Per Serving):
Calories: 350 kcal
Protein: 25 g
Fats: 15 g
Carbs: 30 g

DIRECTIONS

In a large skillet, heat 1 tablespoon of olive oil over medium-high heat. Add the sliced beef and cook for 3-4 minutes, or until browned and cooked through. Remove the beef from the skillet and set aside. In the same skillet, add the remaining tablespoon of olive oil. Add the sliced bell peppers and onion, and sauté for 5-6 minutes, or until they are tender and slightly caramelized. Add the minced garlic, chili powder, ground cumin, paprika, salt, and pepper to the skillet with the veggies. Stir well to combine and cook for an additional 1-2 minutes, until fragrant. Return the cooked beef to the skillet with the veggies, and squeeze the lime juice over the mixture. Stir everything together and cook for another 2-3 minutes to heat through. Warm the flour tortillas according to package instructions. To serve, spoon the beef and veggie mixture onto the warm tortillas. Add optional toppings such as salsa, guacamole, sour cream, or shredded cheese if desired.
Roll up the tortillas and serve immediately.
Enjoy your delicious and flavorful Mexican beef fajitas with sautéed veggies!

37. Vegetable Lasagna with Meaty Tomato Sauce

Yield: 6 servings   Cooking time: 75 min

INGREDIENTS

For the Meaty Tomato Sauce:
- 1 tablespoon olive oil (15ml)
- 1 onion, finely chopped
- 2 cloves garlic, minced
- 500g lean ground beef or turkey
- 400g canned crushed tomatoes
- 2 tablespoons tomato paste (30g)
- 1 teaspoon dried oregano
- 1 teaspoon dried basil
- Salt and pepper to taste

For the Vegetable Filling:
- 2 zucchinis, thinly sliced
- 1 large carrot, thinly sliced
- 1 red bell pepper, thinly sliced
- 200g baby spinach
- Salt and pepper to taste

Other Ingredients:
- 200g lasagna noodles, cooked according to package instructions
- 1 cup low-fat ricotta cheese (250g)
- 1 cup shredded mozzarella cheese (120g)
- Fresh basil leaves for garnish

Nutritional Information (Per Serving):
Calories 320 kcal
Proteins: 25 g
Fats: 12 g
Carbs: 25 g

DIRECTIONS

For the Meaty Tomato Sauce:

Heat olive oil in a large skillet over medium heat. Add the chopped onion and minced garlic, and sauté until softened, about 5 minutes.

Add the ground beef or turkey to the skillet and cook until browned, breaking it up with a spoon.

Stir in the crushed tomatoes, tomato paste, dried oregano, dried basil, salt, and pepper. Simmer for 15-20 minutes, stirring occasionally, until the sauce thickens.

For the Vegetable Filling:

In a separate skillet, heat a little olive oil over medium heat.

Add the sliced zucchinis, carrots, and red bell pepper. Cook until slightly softened, about 5-7 minutes.

Add the baby spinach to the skillet and cook until wilted. Season with salt and pepper to taste.

Assembly:

Preheat the oven to 180°C (350°F).

Spread a thin layer of the meaty tomato sauce on the bottom of a baking dish.

Arrange a layer of cooked lasagna noodles on top of the sauce.

Spread half of the vegetable filling over the noodles, followed by a layer of ricotta cheese and a layer of shredded mozzarella cheese.

Repeat the layers with the remaining ingredients, ending with a layer of meaty tomato sauce on top.

Cover the baking dish with aluminum foil and bake in the preheated oven for 30 minutes.

Remove the foil and bake for an additional 10-15 minutes, or until the cheese is melted and bubbly.

Let the lasagna cool for a few minutes before serving. Garnish with fresh basil leaves, if desired.

Chapter 4: Dinner Delights

Welcome to Chapter 4: Dinner Delights! This section is packed with flavorful recipes designed to elevate your evening meals. Whether you're craving comforting classics or adventurous new flavors, you'll find something here to tantalize your taste buds. Let's explore the art of dinner together and create unforgettable dining experiences right in your own kitchen!

38. Grilled Lemon Herb Chicken with Roasted Vegetables

Yield: 4 servings   Cooking time: 60 min

INGREDIENTS

4 boneless, skinless chicken breasts (600g)
60ml olive oil
2 cloves garlic, minced
Juice and zest of 1 lemon
1 teaspoon dried thyme
1 teaspoon dried rosemary
Salt and pepper to taste
500g mixed vegetables (such as bell peppers, zucchini, and cherry tomatoes)
Fresh parsley, chopped, for garnish

Nutritional Information (Per Serving):
Calories : 300 kcal
Proteins: 30 g
Fats: 12 g
Carbs: 15 g

DIRECTIONS

In a small bowl, whisk together the olive oil, minced garlic, lemon juice, lemon zest, dried thyme, dried rosemary, salt, and pepper.
Place the chicken breasts in a shallow dish and pour the marinade over them. Ensure the chicken is coated evenly.
Marinate for at least 30 minutes in the refrigerator.
Preheat the grill to medium-high heat.
While the chicken is marinating, prepare the vegetables. Chop them into bite-sized pieces.
Thread the marinated chicken onto skewers.
Grill the chicken skewers for 6-8 minutes per side, or until cooked through and juices run clear.
While the chicken is grilling, spread the vegetables out on a baking sheet lined with parchment paper. Drizzle with a little olive oil, salt, and pepper.
Roast the vegetables in the oven at 200°C (400°F) for 15-20 minutes, or until tender and lightly browned.
Once the chicken is done grilling and the vegetables are roasted, serve the chicken skewers alongside the roasted vegetables.
Garnish with freshly chopped parsley before serving

39. Quinoa Stuffed Bell Peppers with Turkey

Yield: 4 servings Cooking time: 60 min

INGREDIENTS

4 large bell peppers
200g lean ground turkey
185g (1 cup) cooked quinoa
1 small onion, finely chopped
2 cloves garlic, minced
5ml (1 teaspoon) olive oil
5ml (1 teaspoon) dried oregano
5ml (1 teaspoon) paprika
Salt and pepper to taste
200g canned diced tomatoes
60g (1/2 cup) shredded mozzarella cheese
Fresh parsley, chopped, for garnish

Nutritional Information
(Per Serving):
Calories 320 kcal
Proteins: 20 g
Fats: 8 g
Carbs: 40 g

DIRECTIONS

Preheat oven to 180°C (350°F).
Prepare bell peppers by cutting off tops, removing seeds and membranes, and placing them in a baking dish.
In a skillet, sauté chopped onion and minced garlic in olive oil until softened (3-4 minutes).
Add ground turkey to the skillet and cook until browned.
Stir in cooked quinoa, dried oregano, paprika, salt, pepper, and diced tomatoes. Cook for 2-3 minutes.
Fill hollowed-out bell peppers with turkey and quinoa mixture.
Cover baking dish with foil and bake for 30 minutes.
Remove foil, sprinkle shredded mozzarella cheese over peppers, and bake for additional 10 minutes until cheese melts.
Garnish with chopped parsley before serving.

40. Baked Cod with Tomato and Olive Relish

Yield: 4 servings Cooking time: 45 min

INGREDIENTS

4 cod fillets (about 600g)
2 tablespoons olive oil
2 cloves garlic, minced
200g cherry tomatoes, halved
50g black olives, sliced
1 tablespoon capers, drained
1 tablespoon fresh lemon juice
1 teaspoon dried oregano
Salt and pepper to taste
Fresh parsley, chopped, for garnish

Nutritional Information
(Per Serving):
Calories: 220 kcal
Protein: 25g
Carbohydrates: 10g
Fat: 5 g

DIRECTIONS

Preheat the oven to 200°C (400°F).
Place the cod fillets in a baking dish and drizzle with olive oil. Season with minced garlic, salt, and pepper.
In a separate bowl, mix together the cherry tomatoes, black olives, capers, lemon juice, and dried oregano. Season with salt and pepper to taste.
Spoon the tomato and olive relish over the cod fillets.
Cover the baking dish with aluminum foil and bake in the preheated oven for 15 minutes.
After 15 minutes, remove the foil and bake for an additional 5 minutes, or until the cod is cooked through and flakes easily with a fork.
Once cooked, remove from the oven and garnish with freshly chopped parsley before serving.

41. Spinach and Mushroom Frittata with Sweet Potato Hash

Yield: 4 servings   Cooking time: 50 min

INGREDIENTS

For the frittata:
6 large eggs, 100g baby spinach leaves
150g mushrooms, sliced
1 small onion, finely chopped
2 cloves garlic, minced
50g feta cheese, crumbled
2 tablespoons olive oil, salt and pepper
Fresh parsley, chopped, for garnish
For the sweet potato hash:
2 medium sweet potatoes, peeled and diced
1 tablespoon olive oil, 1 teaspoon paprika
1/2 teaspoon garlic powder
Salt and pepper to taste

Nutritional Information
(Per Serving):
Calories 280 kcal
Proteins: 10 g
Fats: 15 g
Carbs: 25 g

DIRECTIONS

Preheat oven to 200°C (400°F). Toss diced sweet potatoes with olive oil, paprika, garlic powder, salt, and pepper in a bowl. Spread sweet potatoes on a baking sheet lined with parchment paper and bake for 20-25 minutes until golden and tender, flipping halfway. Whisk eggs with salt and pepper in a large mixing bowl. Heat olive oil in a non-stick skillet over medium heat. Sauté chopped onion and minced garlic until softened (3-4 minutes). Add sliced mushrooms and cook until browned (5-6 minutes). Then add baby spinach and cook until wilted (2 minutes). Pour whisked eggs over vegetables in skillet. Sprinkle crumbled feta cheese on top. Cook frittata over medium-low heat for 8-10 minutes until edges are set but center is slightly runny. Preheat broiler. Place skillet under broiler for 2-3 minutes until top is set and lightly golden. Let cool for a few minutes, then slice into wedges and serve with sweet potato hash. Garnish with freshly chopped parsley before serving.

42. Zucchini Noodles with Pesto and Cherry Tomatoes

Yield: 4 servings   Cooking time: 25 min

INGREDIENTS

For the zucchini noodles:
4 medium zucchini (about 800g)
2 tablespoons (30ml) olive oil
Salt and pepper to taste
For the pesto:
2 cups (40g) fresh basil leaves
1/4 cup (60ml) olive oil
1/4 cup (25g) grated Parmesan cheese
1/4 cup (30g) pine nuts
2 cloves garlic, minced
Salt and pepper to taste
For the cherry tomatoes:
1 cup (150g) cherry tomatoes, halved

Nutritional Information
(Per Serving):
Calories: 200 kcal
Protein: 5g
Carbohydrates: 15g
Fat: 10 g

DIRECTIONS

Use a spiralizer to make zucchini noodles from the zucchini. Set aside.

In a blender or food processor, combine the basil leaves, olive oil, Parmesan cheese, pine nuts, garlic, salt, and pepper. Blend until smooth to make the pesto.

Heat olive oil in a large skillet over medium heat. Add the zucchini noodles and sauté for 2-3 minutes until slightly softened.

Add the cherry tomatoes to the skillet and cook for another 1-2 minutes until they start to soften.

Stir in the pesto sauce and toss until the zucchini noodles and cherry tomatoes are evenly coated.

Cook for an additional 1-2 minutes until heated through. Season with additional salt and pepper to taste if needed. Serve hot, garnished with extra Parmesan cheese and fresh basil leaves if desired.

43. Teriyaki Tofu with Broccoli and Jasmine Rice

Yield: 4 servings   Cooking time: 35 min

INGREDIENTS

For the teriyaki tofu:
400g firm tofu, drained and pressed
1/4 cup (60ml) soy sauce,
2 tablespoons (30ml) honey
2 tablespoons (30ml) rice vinegar
1 clove garlic, minced, 1 teaspoon grated ginger
1 tablespoon (15ml) sesame oil,
1 tablespoon (15ml) cornstarch
2 tablespoons (30ml) water
1 tablespoon (15ml) vegetable oil
For the broccoli:
2 cups (300g) broccoli florets
1 tablespoon (15ml) vegetable oil
Salt and pepper to taste
For the jasmine rice:
1 cup (180g) jasmine rice, 2 cups (480ml) water

Nutritional Information
(Per Serving):
Calories 280 kcal
Proteins: 10 g
Fats: 15 g
Carbs: 25 g

DIRECTIONS

Prepare the jasmine rice according to package instructions.
Cut the tofu into cubes and pat dry with paper towels.
In a small bowl, whisk together the soy sauce, honey, rice vinegar, garlic, ginger, sesame oil, cornstarch, and water to make the teriyaki sauce.
Heat vegetable oil in a large skillet over medium heat. Add the tofu cubes and cook until golden brown on all sides, about 5-7 minutes.
Pour the teriyaki sauce over the tofu and stir to coat. Cook for another 2-3 minutes until the sauce thickens and coats the tofu.
In another skillet, heat vegetable oil over medium heat. Add the broccoli florets and cook for 3-4 minutes until tender-crisp. Season with salt and pepper to taste.
Serve the teriyaki tofu and broccoli over jasmine rice.
Garnish with sesame seeds and chopped green onions if desired.

44. Cauliflower Crust Pizza with Mediterranean Toppings

Yield: 4 servings   Cooking time: 45 min

INGREDIENTS

For the cauliflower crust:
1 medium cauliflower head (about 600g), grated
1/2 cup (50g) grated Parmesan cheese
1/2 cup (50g) mozzarella cheese, shredded
1 egg, 1 teaspoon dried oregano
1/2 teaspoon garlic powder, Salt and pepper
For the toppings:
1/2 cup (120ml) tomato sauce or marinara sauce
1/2 cup (60g) sliced black olives
1/2 cup (75g) sliced cherry tomatoes
1/4 cup (30g) crumbled feta cheese
1/4 cup (25g) sliced red onion
Handful of fresh basil leaves, olive oil for drizzling

Nutritional Information
(Per Serving):
Calories: 200 kcal
Protein: 5g
Carbohydrates: 15g
Fat: 10 g

DIRECTIONS

Preheat oven to 220°C (425°F) and line a baking sheet with parchment paper. Microwave grated cauliflower in a bowl on high for 5-6 minutes until softened, then let it cool slightly. Transfer cooked cauliflower to a clean kitchen towel and squeeze out excess moisture. In a large mixing bowl, combine squeezed cauliflower with Parmesan cheese, mozzarella cheese, egg, oregano, garlic powder, salt, and pepper. Spread cauliflower mixture on prepared baking sheet, shaping it into a round pizza crust about 1/4 inch thick. Bake crust for 20-25 minutes until golden brown and crisp around edges. Remove crust from oven and spread tomato sauce evenly over surface. Arrange olives, cherry tomatoes, feta cheese, red onion slices, and basil leaves on top of sauce. Drizzle with olive oil and return pizza to oven. Bake for 5-7 minutes until toppings are heated through. Slice pizza into wedges and serve hot.

45. Eggplant Parmesan with Whole Grain Garlic Bread

Yield: 4 servings Cooking time: 60 min

INGREDIENTS

For the eggplant parmesan:
2 large eggplants, sliced into rounds
2 eggs, beaten
1 cup (100g) breadcrumbs
1/2 cup (50g) grated Parmesan cheese
2 cups (480ml) marinara sauce
1 cup (120g) shredded mozzarella cheese
Fresh basil leaves for garnish
Salt and pepper to taste
For the whole grain garlic bread:
4 slices whole grain bread
2 tablespoons (30ml) olive oil
2 cloves garlic, minced
1 tablespoon (15ml) chopped fresh parsley
Salt and pepper to taste

Nutritional Information
(Per Serving):
Calories 380 kcal
Proteins: 15 g
Fats: 15 g
Carbs: 45 g

DIRECTIONS

Preheat oven to 200°C (400°F) and line a baking sheet with parchment paper. Place beaten eggs in a shallow dish. In another shallow dish, mix breadcrumbs with grated Parmesan cheese. Dip eggplant slices in beaten eggs, then coat with breadcrumb mixture, pressing gently to adhere. Arrange coated eggplant slices on prepared baking sheet. Bake for 20-25 minutes until golden and crispy.

Meanwhile, prepare whole grain garlic bread. Mix olive oil, minced garlic, chopped parsley, salt, and pepper in a small bowl. Brush olive oil mixture onto each slice of whole grain bread. Place bread slices on separate baking sheet and bake for 5-7 minutes until lightly toasted. Remove eggplant slices from oven and top each with marinara sauce and shredded mozzarella cheese. Return eggplant to oven and bake for 10-15 minutes until cheese is melted and bubbly.

Serve hot, garnished with fresh basil leaves, alongside whole grain garlic bread.

46. Thai Coconut Curry with Tofu and Vegetables

Yield: 4 servings Cooking time: 35 min

INGREDIENTS

1 tablespoon (15ml) vegetable oil
200g tofu, diced, 1 onion, sliced
2 cloves garlic, minced
1 red bell pepper, sliced (150g)
1 green bell pepper, sliced (150g)
1 carrot, sliced (100g), 1 zucchini, sliced (200g)
200g broccoli florets
2 tablespoons (30g) Thai red curry paste
1 can (400ml) coconut milk
1 tablespoon (15ml) soy sauce
1 tablespoon (15ml) lime juice
1 tablespoon (15ml) maple syrup or brown sugar
Fresh cilantro leaves for garnish
Cooked rice or noodles for serving

Nutritional Information
(Per Serving):
Calories: 300 kcal
Protein: 10g
Carbohydrates: 20g
Fat: 25 g

DIRECTIONS

Heat vegetable oil in a large skillet or wok over medium-high heat. Add the diced tofu and cook until golden brown on all sides. Remove from the skillet and set aside.

In the same skillet, add the sliced onion and minced garlic. Cook for 2-3 minutes until softened and fragrant.

Add the sliced bell peppers, carrot, zucchini, and broccoli florets to the skillet. Stir-fry for 5-6 minutes until the vegetables are tender-crisp. Stir in the Thai red curry paste and cook for 1 minute until fragrant. Pour in the coconut milk, soy sauce, lime juice, and maple syrup or brown sugar. Stir to combine and bring the mixture to a simmer.

Add the cooked tofu back to the skillet and simmer for another 2-3 minutes to allow the flavors to meld. Taste and adjust the seasoning with more soy sauce, lime juice, or sweetener if needed. Serve the Thai coconut curry hot over cooked rice or noodles. Garnish with fresh cilantro leaves before serving.

47. Lemon Garlic Salmon with Steamed Asparagus

Yield: 4 servings Cooking time: 25 min

INGREDIENTS

4 salmon fillets (about 150g each)
2 tablespoons (30ml) olive oil
4 cloves garlic, minced
Zest of 1 lemon
Juice of 1 lemon
Salt and pepper to taste
500g asparagus spears, ends trimmed
Lemon wedges for serving

Nutritional Information (Per Serving):
Calories 300 kcal
Proteins: 25 g
Fats: 20 g
Carbs: 5 g

DIRECTIONS

Preheat the oven to 200°C (400°F). Line a baking sheet with parchment paper.
Place the salmon fillets on the prepared baking sheet.
In a small bowl, whisk together the olive oil, minced garlic, lemon zest, lemon juice, salt, and pepper.
Drizzle the lemon garlic mixture over the salmon fillets, ensuring they are evenly coated.
Bake the salmon in the preheated oven for 12-15 minutes, or until cooked through and easily flakes with a fork.
While the salmon is baking, steam the asparagus spears until tender, about 5-7 minutes.
Serve the lemon garlic salmon hot, with steamed asparagus on the side.
Garnish with lemon wedges and fresh herbs if desired.

48. Beef and Broccoli Stir-Fry with Quinoa

Yield: 4 servings Cooking time: 30 min

INGREDIENTS

400g beef sirloin or flank steak, thinly sliced
2 tablespoons (30ml) soy sauce
1 tablespoon (15ml) oyster sauce
1 tablespoon (15ml) hoisin sauce
1 tablespoon (15ml) sesame oil
2 cloves garlic, minced
1 teaspoon (5g) grated ginger
1 tablespoon (15ml) vegetable oil
1 onion, thinly sliced
2 cups (200g) broccoli florets
Cooked quinoa for serving
Sesame seeds for garnish (optional)
Sliced green onions for garnish (optional)

Nutritional Information (Per Serving):
Calories: 350 kcal
Protein: 25g
Carbohydrates: 15g
Fat: 30 g

DIRECTIONS

In a bowl, marinate the thinly sliced beef with soy sauce, oyster sauce, hoisin sauce, sesame oil, minced garlic, and grated ginger. Let it marinate for at least 15 minutes.
Heat vegetable oil in a large skillet or wok over high heat.
Add the marinated beef to the skillet and stir-fry for 2-3 minutes until browned and cooked through. Remove the beef from the skillet and set aside.
In the same skillet, add a bit more oil if needed. Add the thinly sliced onion and broccoli florets. Stir-fry for 3-4 minutes until the vegetables are tender-crisp.
Return the cooked beef to the skillet and toss everything together until heated through.
Serve the beef and broccoli stir-fry hot over cooked quinoa.
Garnish with sesame seeds and sliced green onions if desired.

49. Ratatouille with Herbed Couscous

Yield: 4 servings   Cooking time: 45 min

INGREDIENTS

1 eggplant, diced (300g),
2 zucchinis, diced (300g)
1 red bell pepper, diced (150g)
1 yellow bell pepper, diced (150g)
1 onion, diced (150g), 2 cloves garlic, minced
2 tomatoes, diced (about 300g)
2 tablespoons (30ml) olive oil
1 teaspoon (5g) dried thyme,
1 teaspoon (5g) dried oregano
Salt and pepper to taste, 1 cup (200g) couscous
1 1/4 cups (300ml) vegetable broth or water
Fresh parsley for garnish

Nutritional Information (Per Serving):
Calories: 250 kcal
Proteins: 5 g
Fats: 7 g
Carbs: 40 g

DIRECTIONS

In a large skillet, heat olive oil over medium heat. Add the diced onion and garlic, and sauté until softened and fragrant, about 3-4 minutes. Add the diced eggplant, zucchini, bell peppers, and tomatoes to the skillet. Stir well to combine. Season the vegetables with dried thyme, dried oregano, salt, and pepper. Stir again to distribute the seasoning evenly. Cover the skillet and let the vegetables cook over medium heat for 15-20 minutes, stirring occasionally, until they are tender but still hold their shape. While the ratatouille is cooking, prepare the herbed couscous. In a separate saucepan, bring the vegetable broth or water to a boil. Stir in the couscous, cover the saucepan, and remove it from the heat. Let it sit for 5 minutes to allow the couscous to absorb the liquid. Fluff the couscous with a fork and stir in some freshly chopped parsley for added flavor. Once the ratatouille is cooked, serve it hot over the herbed couscous. Garnish with additional fresh parsley if desired.

50. Stuffed Acorn Squash with Wild Rice and Cranberries

Yield: 4 servings   Cooking time: 60 min

INGREDIENTS

2 acorn squashes, halved and seeds removed
1 cup (200g) wild rice, cooked
1/2 cup (75g) dried cranberries
1/4 cup (30g) chopped pecans
1 small onion, finely chopped (about 100g)
2 cloves garlic, minced
2 tablespoons (30ml) olive oil
1 teaspoon (5g) dried thyme
Salt and pepper to taste
Fresh parsley for garnish

Nutritional Information (Per Serving):
Calories: 300 kcal
Protein: 6g
Carbohydrates: 9g
Fat: 50 g

DIRECTIONS

Preheat the oven to 200°C (400°F). Place the acorn squash halves cut-side down on a baking sheet lined with parchment paper. Bake for 20-25 minutes until the squash is tender but still holds its shape. In a large skillet, heat olive oil over medium heat. Add the chopped onion and minced garlic, and sauté until softened and fragrant, about 3-4 minutes. Add the cooked wild rice, dried cranberries, chopped pecans, dried thyme, salt, and pepper to the skillet. Stir well to combine and cook for another 2-3 minutes to allow the flavors to meld. Remove the skillet from the heat. Carefully flip the baked acorn squash halves over and stuff each half with the wild rice mixture, packing it gently. Return the stuffed acorn squash halves to the oven and bake for another 15-20 minutes until heated through and slightly golden on top.
Serve the stuffed acorn squash hot, garnished with fresh parsley if desired.

51. Chicken Enchilada Casserole with Black Beans and Corn

Yield: 4 servings   Cooking time: 50 min

INGREDIENTS

2 cups (300g) shredded cooked chicken breast
1 can (15 ounces) black beans, drained and rinsed (about 425g)
1 cup (150g) frozen corn kernels
1 cup (240ml) enchilada sauce
1/2 cup (60g) diced red bell pepper
1/2 cup (60g) diced green bell pepper
1/2 cup (50g) diced onion
1 teaspoon (5g) chili powder
1/2 teaspoon (2.5g) ground cumin
Salt and pepper to taste
6 corn tortillas
1 cup (100g) shredded cheddar cheese
Fresh cilantro for garnish

Nutritional Information
(Per Serving):
Calories 325 kcal
Proteins: 25 g
Fats: 10 g
Carbs: 40 g

DIRECTIONS

Preheat the oven to 180°C (350°F). Lightly grease a 9x13-inch baking dish. In a large mixing bowl, combine the shredded chicken, black beans, corn kernels, enchilada sauce, diced bell peppers, diced onion, chili powder, ground cumin, salt, and pepper. Mix well to combine. Place 2 corn tortillas on the bottom of the prepared baking dish, overlapping slightly to cover the bottom. Spoon half of the chicken and bean mixture over the tortillas, spreading it evenly. Place 2 more tortillas on top of the chicken mixture, followed by the remaining chicken and bean mixture. Top with the remaining 2 tortillas and sprinkle the shredded cheddar cheese over the top. Cover the baking dish with foil and bake in the preheated oven for 20 minutes.
Remove the foil and continue baking for another 10 minutes, or until the cheese is melted and bubbly.
Remove from the oven and let it cool for a few minutes before serving.
Garnish with fresh cilantro before serving.

52. Mushroom Risotto with Peas and Parmesan

Yield: 4 servings   Cooking time: 40 min

INGREDIENTS

1 cup (200g) Arborio rice
4 cups (960ml) vegetable broth
2 tablespoons (30ml) olive oil
1 onion, finely chopped (about 100g)
2 cloves garlic, minced
8 ounces (225g) mushrooms, sliced
1 cup (150g) frozen peas
1/2 cup (50g) grated Parmesan cheese
Salt and pepper to taste
Fresh parsley for garnish

Nutritional Information
(Per Serving):
Calories: 350 kcal
Protein: 10g
Carbohydrates: 10 g
Fat: 50 g

DIRECTIONS

Heat vegetable broth in a saucepan over medium heat until simmering, then reduce heat to low to keep warm.
In a large skillet or Dutch oven, heat olive oil over medium heat. Add onion and garlic, sauté until softened, about 3-4 minutes. Add mushrooms to skillet, cook until golden brown and tender, about 5-6 minutes.
Stir in Arborio rice, cook for 2-3 minutes until lightly toasted. Begin adding warm vegetable broth to skillet, one ladleful at a time, stirring constantly, until rice is creamy and cooked through, about 20-25 minutes.
Add frozen peas during last 5 minutes of cooking, allowing them to heat through.
Remove skillet from heat. Stir in grated Parmesan cheese until melted and blended.
Season with salt and pepper to taste.
Serve hot, garnished with fresh parsley.

53. Lentil Curry with Cauliflower Rice

Yield: 4 servings	Cooking time: 45 min

INGREDIENTS

For the lentil curry:
- 200g dried green lentils
- 1 tbsp olive oil
- 1 onion, finely chopped
- 2 cloves garlic, minced
- 1 tbsp ginger, minced
- 1 tbsp curry powder
- 1 tsp ground cumin
- 1 tsp ground coriander
- 1/2 tsp turmeric powder
- 400g canned diced tomatoes
- 400ml canned coconut milk
- 200g baby spinach leaves
- Salt and pepper to taste
- Fresh cilantro, chopped, for garnish

For the cauliflower rice:
- 1 medium head cauliflower
- 1 tbsp olive oil
- Salt and pepper to taste

DIRECTIONS

For the lentil curry:
Rinse lentils and set aside.
Heat olive oil in a pot, sauté onion, garlic, and ginger until fragrant.
Add spices, lentils, tomatoes, and coconut milk. Simmer for 20-25 minutes.
Stir in spinach until wilted. Season with salt and pepper.
Garnish with cilantro.

For the cauliflower rice:
Grate cauliflower into rice-like texture.
Sauté cauliflower rice with olive oil until tender.
Season with salt and pepper.
Serve lentil curry over cauliflower rice.

Nutritional Information (Per Serving):
Calories 320 kcal
Proteins: 25 g
Fats: 12 g
Carbs: 25 g

54. Turkey Meatballs in Marinara Sauce with Whole Wheat Spaghetti

Yield: 4 servings   Cooking time: 50 min

INGREDIENTS

For the turkey meatballs:
- 500g lean ground turkey
- 1/4 cup (25g) breadcrumbs
- 1/4 cup (20g) grated Parmesan cheese
- 1 egg
- 2 cloves garlic, minced
- 1 tablespoon (15ml) olive oil
- 1/2 teaspoon dried oregano
- 1/2 teaspoon dried basil
- Salt and pepper to taste

For the marinara sauce:
- 2 cups (500ml) canned crushed tomatoes
- 2 cloves garlic, minced
- 1 tablespoon (15ml) olive oil
- 1 teaspoon dried basil
- 1 teaspoon dried oregano
- Salt and pepper to taste

For the whole wheat spaghetti:
- 320g whole wheat spaghetti
- Salt for boiling water

Nutritional Information (Per Serving):
Calories 320 kcal
Proteins: 25 g
Fats: 12 g
Carbs: 25 g

DIRECTIONS

Preheat the oven to 200°C (400°F) and line a baking sheet with parchment paper.

In a large bowl, combine the ground turkey, breadcrumbs, Parmesan cheese, egg, minced garlic, olive oil, dried oregano, dried basil, salt, and pepper. Mix until well combined.

Shape the turkey mixture into meatballs, about 1 inch in diameter, and place them on the prepared baking sheet.

Bake the meatballs in the preheated oven for 15-20 minutes until cooked through and lightly browned.

While the meatballs are baking, prepare the marinara sauce.

Heat olive oil in a large skillet over medium heat. Add the minced garlic and cook for 1-2 minutes until fragrant.

Stir in the crushed tomatoes, dried basil, dried oregano, salt, and pepper. Simmer the sauce for 10-15 minutes, stirring occasionally.

Cook the whole wheat spaghetti according to package instructions in a large pot of salted boiling water until al dente. Drain and set aside.

Once the meatballs are cooked, add them to the marinara sauce and gently toss to coat.

Serve the turkey meatballs and marinara sauce over cooked whole wheat spaghetti.

Garnish with freshly chopped parsley and grated Parmesan cheese if desired.

55. Sweet and Sour Pork Stir-Fry with Pineapple

Yield: 4 servings   Cooking time: 30 min

INGREDIENTS

For the sweet and sour sauce:
- 1/4 cup (60ml) soy sauce
- 1/4 cup (60ml) rice vinegar
- 2 tablespoons (30ml) honey
- 2 tablespoons (30ml) ketchup
- 1 tablespoon (15ml) cornstarch
- 1/4 cup (60ml) water

For the stir-fry:
- 500g lean pork tenderloin, thinly sliced
- 1 tablespoon (15ml) vegetable oil
- 2 cloves garlic, minced
- 1 red bell pepper, sliced
- 1 green bell pepper, sliced
- 1 cup (150g) pineapple chunks (fresh or canned)
- Salt and pepper to taste
- Cooked rice for serving

DIRECTIONS

In a small bowl, whisk together the soy sauce, rice vinegar, honey, ketchup, cornstarch, and water to make the sweet and sour sauce. Set aside.

Heat vegetable oil in a large skillet or wok over high heat.

Add the minced garlic and cook for 1 minute until fragrant.

Add the sliced pork to the skillet and stir-fry for 2-3 minutes until browned.

Add the sliced bell peppers to the skillet and continue to stir-fry for another 2-3 minutes until they start to soften.

Stir in the pineapple chunks and cook for 1-2 minutes until heated through.

Pour the sweet and sour sauce over the pork and vegetables in the skillet. Stir well to coat everything evenly.

Cook for an additional 1-2 minutes until the sauce thickens and coats the ingredients.

Season with salt and pepper to taste.

Serve the sweet and sour pork stir-fry hot over cooked rice.

Nutritional Information (Per Serving):
Calories 350 kcal
Proteins: 25 g
Fats: 10 g
Carbs: 35 g

Chapter 5: Nourishing Salads

In this chapter, we explore the vibrant world of salads – a delightful and nutritious way to enjoy a variety of fresh ingredients packed with flavor and nutrients. From crisp green salads to hearty grain-based bowls, each recipe offers a satisfying balance of textures, flavors, and nutrients. Whether you're a devoted salad lover or new to the world of leafy greens, there's something here for everyone to enjoy. So grab your bowl, mix up some dressing, and let's dive into the wonderful world of nourishing salads!

56. Greek Salad with Lemon Herb Dressing

Yield: 4 servings   Cooking time: 15 min

INGREDIENTS

2 cups (200 g) chopped romaine lettuce
1 cucumber (about 300 g), diced
1 cup (150 g) cherry tomatoes, halved
1/2 cup (75 g) sliced red onion
1/2 cup (75 g) sliced Kalamata olives
1/2 cup (75 g) crumbled feta cheese
Fresh parsley for garnish
Lemon Herb Dressing:
1/4 cup (60 ml) extra virgin olive oil
Juice of 1 lemon, 2 cloves garlic, minced
1 teaspoon (5 ml) dried oregano
1 teaspoon (5 ml) dried basil
Salt and pepper to taste

Nutritional Information
(Per Serving):
Calories : 300 kcal
Proteins: 30 g
Fats: 12 g
Carbs: 15 g

DIRECTIONS

In a large salad bowl, combine the chopped romaine lettuce, diced cucumber, cherry tomatoes, sliced red onion, and Kalamata olives.

In a small bowl, whisk together the extra virgin olive oil, lemon juice, minced garlic, dried oregano, dried basil, salt, and pepper to make the dressing.

Pour the dressing over the salad and toss until everything is evenly coated.

Sprinkle the crumbled feta cheese over the top of the salad.

Garnish with fresh parsley.

Serve immediately and enjoy your refreshing Greek salad with lemon herb dressing!

57. Caprese Salad with Balsamic Glaze

Yield: 4 servings   Cooking time: 10 min

INGREDIENTS

2 large tomatoes (about 300 g), sliced
1 ball fresh mozzarella cheese (about 200 g), sliced
1/4 cup (60 ml) balsamic glaze
Fresh basil leaves for garnish
Salt and pepper to taste

DIRECTIONS

Arrange the tomato and mozzarella slices on a serving platter, alternating them.
Drizzle the balsamic glaze over the tomato and mozzarella slices.
Season with salt and pepper to taste.
Garnish with fresh basil leaves.
Serve immediately as a refreshing appetizer or side dish.

Nutritional Information (Per Serving):
Calories 150 kcal
Proteins: 10 g
Fats: 8 g
Carbs: 10 g

58. Asian Sesame Chicken Salad

Yield: 4 servings   Cooking time: 25 min

INGREDIENTS

2 boneless, skinless chicken breasts (about 400 g), cooked and shredded
4 cups (200 g) mixed salad greens
1 red bell pepper, thinly sliced
1 carrot, julienned
1/4 cup (30 g) sliced almonds, toasted
2 green onions, thinly sliced
Sesame seeds for garnish
Sesame Ginger Dressing:
2 tablespoons (30 ml) soy sauce
1 tablespoon (15 ml) rice vinegar
1 tablespoon (15 ml) sesame oil
1 tablespoon (15 ml) honey
1 teaspoon (5 ml) grated fresh ginger

DIRECTIONS

In a large bowl, combine the cooked and shredded chicken, mixed salad greens, sliced red bell pepper, julienned carrot, sliced almonds, and thinly sliced green onions.
In a small bowl, whisk together the soy sauce, rice vinegar, sesame oil, honey, grated fresh ginger, and minced garlic to make the dressing.
Pour the dressing over the salad and toss until everything is evenly coated.
Garnish with sesame seeds.
Serve immediately as a satisfying and flavorful meal.

Nutritional Information (Per Serving):
Calories: 300 kcal
Proteins: 25 g
Fats: 12 g
Carbs: 20 g

59. Mango Avocado Salad with Chili Lime Dressing

Yield: 4 servings   Cooking time: 15 min

INGREDIENTS

2 ripe mangoes (400 g), peeled, pitted
2 ripe avocados (300 g), peeled, pitted
1/4 cup (15 g) chopped fresh cilantro
1/4 cup (30 g) finely chopped red onion
1 jalapeño pepper, seeded and minced
Juice of 2 limes, Zest of 1 lime
Salt and pepper to taste
Chili Lime Dressing:
3 tablespoons (45 ml) extra virgin olive oil
2 tablespoons (30 ml) lime juice
1 teaspoon (5 ml) honey
1/2 teaspoon (2.5 ml) chili powder
1/4 teaspoon (1.25 ml) ground cumin
Salt and pepper to taste

Nutritional Information (Per Serving):
Calories 150 kcal
Proteins: 10 g
Fats: 8 g
Carbs: 10 g

DIRECTIONS

In a large bowl, combine the diced mangoes, diced avocados, chopped fresh cilantro, finely chopped red onion, and minced jalapeño pepper.

In a small bowl, whisk together the extra virgin olive oil, lime juice, honey, chili powder, ground cumin, salt, and pepper to make the dressing.

Pour the dressing over the salad and toss gently until everything is evenly coated.

Garnish with lime zest.

Serve immediately as a refreshing and vibrant salad.

60. Cobb Salad with Creamy Avocado Dressing

Yield: 4 servings   Cooking time: 20 min

INGREDIENTS

4 cups (200 g) mixed salad greens
2 boneless, skinless chicken breasts (about 400 g), grilled and sliced
4 hard-boiled eggs, sliced
1 avocado (about 200 g), diced
1 cup (150 g) cherry tomatoes, halved
1/2 cup (75 g) crumbled blue cheese
4 slices cooked bacon, crumbled
Salt and pepper to taste
Creamy Avocado Dressing:
1 ripe avocado (about 200 g)
1/4 cup (60 ml) Greek yogurt
2 tablespoons (30 ml) lime juice
1 garlic clove, minced
2 tablespoons (30 ml) extra virgin olive oil
Salt and pepper to taste

Nutritional Information (Per Serving):
Calories: 300 kcal
Proteins: 25 g
Fats: 12 g
Carbs: 20 g

DIRECTIONS

In a large salad bowl, arrange the mixed salad greens.

Top the greens with sliced grilled chicken, hard-boiled egg slices, diced avocado, cherry tomato halves, crumbled blue cheese, and crumbled bacon.

To make the creamy avocado dressing, combine the ripe avocado, Greek yogurt, lime juice, minced garlic, extra virgin olive oil, salt, and pepper in a blender. Blend until smooth and creamy.

Drizzle the creamy avocado dressing over the salad.

Season with salt and pepper to taste.

Serve immediately as a hearty and satisfying salad.

61. Roasted Beet and Goat Cheese Salad

Yield: 4 servings   Cooking time: 45 min

INGREDIENTS

4 medium-sized beets (about 500 g), peeled and diced
4 cups (200 g) mixed salad greens
1/2 cup (75 g) crumbled goat cheese
1/4 cup (30 g) chopped walnuts, toasted
2 tablespoons (30 ml) balsamic vinegar
2 tablespoons (30 ml) extra virgin olive oil
Salt and pepper to taste

Nutritional Information (Per Serving):
Calories 220 kcal
Proteins: 7 g
Fats: 15 g
Carbs: 17 g

DIRECTIONS

Preheat the oven to 400°F (200°C).
Place the diced beets on a baking sheet lined with parchment paper. Drizzle with 1 tablespoon of olive oil and season with salt and pepper. Toss to coat evenly.
Roast the beets in the preheated oven for about 30-35 minutes, or until tender and caramelized, stirring halfway through.
In a large salad bowl, combine the mixed salad greens, roasted beets, crumbled goat cheese, and toasted chopped walnuts.
In a small bowl, whisk together the balsamic vinegar and remaining olive oil to make the dressing.
Drizzle the dressing over the salad and toss gently to combine.
Season with additional salt and pepper to taste, if desired.
Serve immediately as a delicious and colorful salad.

62. Spinach Strawberry Salad with Poppy Seed Dressing

Yield: 4 servings   Cooking time: 15 min

INGREDIENTS

6 cups (180 g) fresh baby spinach leaves
1 cup (150 g) sliced strawberries
1/4 cup (30 g) sliced almonds, toasted
1/4 cup (30 g) crumbled feta cheese (optional)
2 tablespoons (30 ml) balsamic vinegar
1 tablespoon (15 ml) honey
1 teaspoon (5 ml) Dijon mustard
2 tablespoons (30 ml) extra virgin olive oil
1 teaspoon (5 ml) poppy seeds
Salt and pepper to taste

Nutritional Information (Per Serving):
Calories: 180 kcal
Proteins: 4 g
Fats: 12 g
Carbs: 16 g

DIRECTIONS

In a large salad bowl, combine the fresh baby spinach leaves, sliced strawberries, toasted sliced almonds, and crumbled feta cheese.
In a small bowl, whisk together the balsamic vinegar, honey, Dijon mustard, extra virgin olive oil, poppy seeds, salt, and pepper to make the dressing.
Drizzle the dressing over the salad and toss gently to combine.
Serve immediately as a refreshing and flavorful salad.

63. Mediterranean Chickpea Salad with Feta

Yield: 4 servings Cooking time: 15 min

INGREDIENTS

2 cans (400 g each) chickpeas, drained and rinsed
1 cup (150 g) cherry tomatoes, halved
1 cucumber, diced
1/4 cup (30 g) diced red onion
1/4 cup (15 g) chopped fresh parsley
1/4 cup (15 g) chopped fresh mint leaves
1/4 cup (60 g) crumbled feta cheese
Juice of 1 lemon
2 tablespoons (30 ml) extra virgin olive oil
Salt and pepper to taste

Nutritional Information (Per Serving):
Calories 280 kcal
Proteins: 10 g
Fats: 10 g
Carbs: 35 g

DIRECTIONS

In a large salad bowl, combine the chickpeas, cherry tomatoes, diced cucumber, diced red onion, chopped fresh parsley, and chopped fresh mint leaves.
Crumble the feta cheese over the salad ingredients.
Drizzle the lemon juice and extra virgin olive oil over the salad.
Season with salt and pepper to taste.
Toss gently to combine all the ingredients.
Serve immediately as a satisfying and flavorful salad.

64. Arugula, Pear, and Walnut Salad with Honey Dijon Dressing

Yield: 4 servings Cooking time: 15 min

INGREDIENTS

6 cups (180 g) arugula leaves
2 ripe pears, thinly sliced
1/2 cup (60 g) chopped walnuts, toasted
1/4 cup (30 g) crumbled blue cheese (optional)
2 tablespoons (30 ml) balsamic vinegar
1 tablespoon (15 ml) honey
1 teaspoon (5 ml) Dijon mustard
2 tablespoons (30 ml) extra virgin olive oil
Salt and pepper to taste

Nutritional Information (Per Serving):
Calories: 220 kcal
Proteins: 4 g
Fats: 14 g
Carbs: 22 g

DIRECTIONS

In a large salad bowl, combine the arugula leaves, thinly sliced pears, toasted chopped walnuts, and crumbled blue cheese (if using).
In a small bowl, whisk together the balsamic vinegar, honey, Dijon mustard, extra virgin olive oil, salt, and pepper to make the dressing.
Drizzle the dressing over the salad.
Toss gently to coat all the ingredients with the dressing.
Serve immediately as a refreshing and flavorful salad.

65. Shrimp and Mango Quinoa Salad

Yield: 4 servings Cooking time: 20 min

INGREDIENTS

1 cup (185 g) quinoa, rinsed and cooked
1 lb (450 g) medium shrimp, peeled and deveined
1 ripe mango, peeled and diced
1 red bell pepper, diced
1/4 cup (15 g) chopped fresh cilantro
1/4 cup (15 g) chopped red onion
Juice of 2 limes
2 tablespoons (30 ml) olive oil
Salt and pepper to taste

Nutritional Information (Per Serving):
Calories 280 kcal
Proteins: 24 g
Fats: 6 g
Carbs: 31 g

DIRECTIONS

Cook the quinoa according to package instructions and let it cool to room temperature.
In a large mixing bowl, combine the cooked quinoa, diced mango, diced red bell pepper, chopped cilantro, and chopped red onion.
In a separate skillet, heat olive oil over medium heat. Add the shrimp and cook for 2-3 minutes on each side until they turn pink and opaque.
Remove the shrimp from the skillet and let them cool slightly.
Add the cooked shrimp to the quinoa mixture.
Squeeze the lime juice over the salad and drizzle with olive oil.
Season with salt and pepper to taste.
Toss gently to combine all the ingredients.
Serve immediately as a delightful and nutritious salad.

66. Mexican Street Corn Salad

Yield: 4 servings Cooking time: 20 min

INGREDIENTS

6 cups (180 g) arugula leaves
2 ripe pears, thinly sliced
1/2 cup (60 g) chopped walnuts, toasted
1/4 cup (30 g) crumbled blue cheese (optional)
2 tablespoons (30 ml) balsamic vinegar
1 tablespoon (15 ml) honey
1 teaspoon (5 ml) Dijon mustard
2 tablespoons (30 ml) extra virgin olive oil
Salt and pepper to taste

Nutritional Information (Per Serving):
Calories: 220 kcal
Proteins: 4 g
Fats: 14 g
Carbs: 22 g

DIRECTIONS

In a large salad bowl, combine the arugula leaves, thinly sliced pears, toasted chopped walnuts, and crumbled blue cheese (if using).
In a small bowl, whisk together the balsamic vinegar, honey, Dijon mustard, extra virgin olive oil, salt, and pepper to make the dressing.
Drizzle the dressing over the salad.
Toss gently to coat all the ingredients with the dressing.
Serve immediately as a refreshing and flavorful salad.

67. Watermelon Feta Salad with Mint

Yield: 4 servings   Cooking time: 15 min

INGREDIENTS

4 cups (600 g) cubed watermelon
1/2 cup (75 g) crumbled feta cheese
1/4 cup (15 g) chopped fresh mint leaves
2 tablespoons (30 ml) balsamic glaze

DIRECTIONS

In a large mixing bowl, combine the cubed watermelon, crumbled feta cheese, and chopped fresh mint leaves.
Drizzle with balsamic glaze.
Season with salt and pepper to taste.
Gently toss to combine all the ingredients.
Serve immediately as a refreshing and delightful salad.

Nutritional Information
(Per Serving):
Calories 120 kcal
Proteins: 3 g
Fats: 4 g
Carbs: 20 g

68. Tuna Niçoise Salad

Yield: 4 servings   Cooking time: 25 min

INGREDIENTS

1 lb (450 g) baby potatoes, halved
8 oz (225 g) green beans, trimmed
4 large eggs
2 cans (280 g total) canned tuna, drained
4 cups (120 g) mixed salad greens
1 cup (150 g) cherry tomatoes, halved
1/2 cup (75 g) sliced black olives
1/4 cup (15 g) chopped fresh parsley
1/4 cup (60 ml) extra virgin olive oil
2 tablespoons (30 ml) red wine vinegar
1 teaspoon (5 ml) Dijon mustard
Salt and pepper to taste

Nutritional Information
(Per Serving):
Calories: 300 kcal
Proteins: 20 g
Fats: 15 g
Carbs: 20 g

DIRECTIONS

In a medium saucepan, boil water and add the baby potatoes. Cook for about 10-12 minutes until tender. Drain and set aside. In the same saucepan, bring another pot of water to boil. Add the green beans and cook for about 3-4 minutes until crisp-tender. Drain and set aside.
In a separate pot, place the eggs and cover them with water. Bring to a boil, then reduce the heat and simmer for about 8-10 minutes for hard-boiled eggs. Once cooked, drain, and rinse with cold water. Peel the eggs and cut them into halves.
In a large salad bowl, arrange the mixed salad greens, cooked baby potatoes, green beans, cherry tomatoes, sliced black olives, and chopped fresh parsley. Top the salad with the canned tuna and boiled egg halves. In a small bowl, whisk together the extra virgin olive oil, red wine vinegar, Dijon mustard, salt, and pepper to make the dressing. Drizzle the dressing over the salad or serve it on the side. Toss gently to coat all the ingredients with the dressing.
Serve immediately as a hearty and satisfying Tuna Niçoise Salad.

69. Broccoli Crunch Salad with Bacon and Sunflower Seeds

Yield: 4 servings   Cooking time: 20 min

INGREDIENTS

4 cups (400 g) broccoli florets
4 slices bacon, cooked and crumbled
1/4 cup (30 g) sunflower seeds
1/4 cup (30 g) dried cranberries
1/4 cup (60 g) diced red onion
1/4 cup (60 g) plain Greek yogurt
2 tablespoons (30 ml) apple cider vinegar
1 tablespoon (15 ml) honey
Salt and pepper to taste

DIRECTIONS

In a large mixing bowl, combine the broccoli florets, crumbled bacon, sunflower seeds, dried cranberries, and diced red onion.

In a small bowl, whisk together the plain Greek yogurt, apple cider vinegar, honey, salt, and pepper to make the dressing.

Pour the dressing over the broccoli mixture.

Toss gently to coat all the ingredients evenly.

Serve immediately as a delicious and nutritious Broccoli Crunch Salad.

Nutritional Information (Per Serving):
Calories: 250 kcal
Proteins: 10 g
Fats: 10 g
Carbs: 30 g

70. Warm Lentil Salad with Roasted Vegetables

Yield: 4 servings   Cooking time: 30 min

INGREDIENTS

1 cup (200 g) green lentils, rinsed
2 cups (480 ml) vegetable broth
2 cups (300 g) diced mixed vegetables (such as bell peppers, carrots, zucchini)
1 red onion, thinly sliced
3 cloves garlic, minced
2 tablespoons (30 ml) olive oil
1 tablespoon (15 ml) balsamic vinegar
1 teaspoon (5 ml) dried thyme
Salt and pepper to taste
Fresh parsley, for garnish

DIRECTIONS

Preheat the oven to 400°F (200°C).

In a medium saucepan, combine the green lentils and vegetable broth. Bring to a boil, then reduce the heat and simmer for 20-25 minutes until the lentils are tender. Drain any excess liquid and set aside.

In a large mixing bowl, toss the diced mixed vegetables, red onion, minced garlic, olive oil, balsamic vinegar, dried thyme, salt, and pepper until evenly coated.

Spread the vegetable mixture in a single layer on a baking sheet lined with parchment paper.

Roast in the preheated oven for 20-25 minutes, stirring halfway through, until the vegetables are tender and slightly caramelized.

In a serving bowl, combine the cooked lentils and roasted vegetables.

Garnish with fresh parsley and serve warm as a hearty and flavorful Warm Lentil Salad with Roasted Vegetables.

Nutritional Information (Per Serving):
Calories: 280 kcal
Proteins: 12 g
Fats: 7 g
Carbs: 42 g

71. Orzo Pasta Salad with Mediterranean Vegetables

Yield: 4 servings			Cooking time: 30 min

INGREDIENTS

1 cup (200 g) orzo pasta
2 cups (480 ml) vegetable broth
1 cup (150 g) cherry tomatoes, halved
1/2 cup (75 g) diced cucumber
1/2 cup (75 g) diced bell pepper (any color)
1/4 cup (30 g) sliced black olives
1/4 cup (30 g) crumbled feta cheese
2 tablespoons (30 ml) extra virgin olive oil
1 tablespoon (15 ml) balsamic vinegar
1 clove garlic, minced
1 teaspoon (5 ml) dried oregano
Salt and pepper to taste
Fresh basil leaves, for garnish

Nutritional Information
(Per Serving):
Calories 280 kcal
Proteins: 7 g
Fats: 10 g
Carbs: 40 g

DIRECTIONS

In a medium saucepan, bring the vegetable broth to a boil. Add the orzo pasta and cook according to package instructions until al dente. Drain and set aside to cool.

In a large mixing bowl, combine the cooked orzo pasta, halved cherry tomatoes, diced cucumber, diced bell pepper, sliced black olives, and crumbled feta cheese.

In a small bowl, whisk together the extra virgin olive oil, balsamic vinegar, minced garlic, dried oregano, salt, and pepper to make the dressing.

Pour the dressing over the pasta and vegetables. Toss gently to coat everything evenly.

Garnish with fresh basil leaves.

Serve immediately as a refreshing and flavorful Orzo Pasta Salad with Mediterranean Vegetables.

72. Apple Walnut Salad with Maple Dijon Vinaigrette

Yield: 4 servings			Cooking time: 15 min

INGREDIENTS

For the salad:
6 cups (180 g) mixed salad greens (such as lettuce, spinach, arugula)
1 large apple, thinly sliced
1/2 cup (60 g) walnuts, roughly chopped
1/4 cup (30 g) dried cranberries
1/4 cup (30 g) crumbled feta cheese (optional)
For the Maple Dijon Vinaigrette:
2 tablespoons (30 ml) olive oil
1 tablespoon (15 ml) apple cider vinegar
1 tablespoon (15 ml) maple syrup
1 teaspoon (5 ml) Dijon mustard
Salt and pepper to taste

Nutritional Information
(Per Serving):
Calories: 250 kcal
Proteins: 4 g
Fats: 17 g
Carbs: 22 g

DIRECTIONS

In a small bowl, whisk together the ingredients for the Maple Dijon Vinaigrette: olive oil, apple cider vinegar, maple syrup, Dijon mustard, salt, and pepper. Set aside.

In a large salad bowl, combine the mixed salad greens, thinly sliced apple, chopped walnuts, dried cranberries, and crumbled feta cheese (if using).

Drizzle the Maple Dijon Vinaigrette over the salad. Toss gently to coat everything evenly.

Serve immediately as a refreshing and nutritious Apple Walnut Salad with Maple Dijon Vinaigrette.

73. Thai Beef Salad with Peanut Dressing

Yield: 4 servings	Cooking time: 25 min

INGREDIENTS

For the salad:
- 1 lb (450 g) beef sirloin or flank steak, thinly sliced
- 8 cups (200 g) mixed salad greens
- 1 cucumber, thinly sliced
- 1 red bell pepper, thinly sliced
- 1/2 cup (75 g) cherry tomatoes, halved
- 1/4 cup (15 g) chopped cilantro
- 1/4 cup (15 g) chopped mint leaves
- 1/4 cup (30 g) chopped roasted peanuts

For the peanut dressing:
- 1/4 cup (60 ml) creamy peanut butter
- 2 tablespoons (30 ml) soy sauce
- 2 tablespoons (30 ml) rice vinegar
- 1 tablespoon (15 ml) lime juice
- 1 tablespoon (15 ml) honey
- 1 teaspoon (5 ml) grated ginger
- 1 clove garlic, minced
- 2 tablespoons (30 ml) water, to thin

DIRECTIONS

In a bowl, whisk together all the ingredients for the peanut dressing until smooth. If the dressing is too thick, add a little water to thin it out. Set aside.

Season the sliced beef with salt and pepper. Heat a skillet over medium-high heat and add a little oil. Cook the beef slices for 2-3 minutes per side, or until cooked to your desired level of doneness. Remove from the skillet and set aside.

In a large mixing bowl, combine the mixed salad greens, sliced cucumber, sliced red bell pepper, halved cherry tomatoes, chopped cilantro, and chopped mint leaves.

Add the cooked beef slices to the salad.

Drizzle the peanut dressing over the salad and toss gently to coat everything evenly.

Sprinkle chopped roasted peanuts on top for extra crunch. Serve immediately as a delicious and vibrant Thai Beef Salad with Peanut Dressing.

Nutritional Information (Per Serving):
Calories 350 kcal
Proteins: 25 g
Fats: 10 g
Carbs: 35 g

74. Roasted Cauliflower and Chickpea Salad with Lemon Tahini Dressing

Yield: 4 servings   Cooking time: 40 min

INGREDIENTS

For the salad:
- 1 head cauliflower, cut into florets
- 1 can (15 oz / 425 g) chickpeas, drained and rinsed
- 2 tablespoons (30 ml) olive oil
- Salt and pepper to taste
- 4 cups (120 g) mixed salad greens
- 1/4 cup (15 g) chopped fresh parsley
- 2 tablespoons (15 g) toasted pine nuts (optional)

For the lemon tahini dressing:
- 1/4 cup (60 ml) tahini
- 2 tablespoons (30 ml) lemon juice
- 1 tablespoon (15 ml) water
- 1 clove garlic, minced
- 1/2 teaspoon (2.5 ml) ground cumin
- Salt and pepper to taste

Nutritional Information (Per Serving):
Calories 320 kcal
Proteins: 11 g
Fats: 18 g
Carbs: 32 g

DIRECTIONS

Preheat the oven to 400°F (200°C).

In a large mixing bowl, toss the cauliflower florets and chickpeas with olive oil, salt, and pepper until evenly coated.

Spread the cauliflower and chickpeas in a single layer on a baking sheet lined with parchment paper.

Roast in the preheated oven for 25-30 minutes, stirring halfway through, until the cauliflower is tender and golden brown.

In the meantime, prepare the lemon tahini dressing by whisking together tahini, lemon juice, water, minced garlic, ground cumin, salt, and pepper in a small bowl until smooth.

If the dressing is too thick, add a little more water to reach the desired consistency.

Once the cauliflower and chickpeas are roasted, remove them from the oven and let them cool slightly.

In a large salad bowl, combine the mixed salad greens, roasted cauliflower, and chickpeas.

Drizzle the lemon tahini dressing over the salad and toss gently to coat everything evenly.

Sprinkle chopped fresh parsley and toasted pine nuts (if using) on top for garnish.

Serve immediately as a hearty and flavorful Roasted Cauliflower and Chickpea Salad with Lemon Tahini Dressing.

Chapter 6: Plant-Based Cuisine

In this chapter, we celebrate the abundance of plant-based ingredients and explore the delicious possibilities they offer. Whether you're a committed vegan or simply looking to incorporate more plant-based meals into your diet, you'll find plenty of inspiration here. From vibrant salads to hearty mains, each recipe showcases the diversity and flavor of plant-based ingredients. Embracing plant-based eating isn't just good for your health; it's also good for the planet. So join us on this journey as we discover the delicious and nutritious world of plant-based cuisine!

75. Quinoa and Black Bean Salad

Yield: 4 servings   Cooking time: 30 min

INGREDIENTS
1 cup (185g) quinoa
2 cups (480ml) water or vegetable broth
1 can (15 oz/425g) black beans, drained and rinsed
1 red bell pepper, diced
1 cup (150g) cherry tomatoes, halved
1/4 cup (15g) chopped fresh cilantro
2 tablespoons (30ml) lime juice
2 tablespoons (30ml) olive oil
1 teaspoon (5g) ground cumin
Salt and pepper to taste
Avocado slices, for serving (optional)

Nutritional Information (Per Serving):
Calories : 280 kcal
Proteins: 10 g
Fats: 8 g
Carbs: 45 g

DIRECTIONS
Rinse the quinoa under cold water. In a saucepan, bring 2 cups of water or vegetable broth to a boil. Add the quinoa, reduce heat to low, cover, and simmer for 15-20 minutes, or until all liquid is absorbed. Remove from heat and let it sit covered for 5 minutes. Fluff with a fork and let cool. In a large mixing bowl, combine the cooked quinoa, black beans, diced red bell pepper, halved cherry tomatoes, and chopped cilantro. In a small bowl, whisk together the lime juice, olive oil, ground cumin, salt, and pepper. Pour the dressing over the quinoa and black bean mixture, tossing gently to coat all ingredients evenly. Taste and adjust seasoning if necessary. Serve the quinoa and black bean salad at room temperature or chilled.
Optionally, garnish with avocado slices before serving.
Enjoy this refreshing and protein-packed Quinoa and Black Bean Salad!

76. Spicy Tofu Stir-Fry

Yield: 4 servings   Cooking time: 25 min

INGREDIENTS

- 1 block (/400g) firm tofu, drained and cubed
- 2 tablespoons (30ml) soy sauce
- 2 tablespoons (30ml) rice vinegar
- 1 tablespoon (15ml) sesame oil
- 2 teaspoons (10g) brown sugar
- 2 tablespoons (30ml) vegetable oil
- 1 onion, thinly sliced, 2 cloves garlic, minced
- 1 bell pepper, thinly sliced
- 1 cup (150g) snap peas, trimmed
- 1 tablespoon (15g) grated ginger
- 2 tablespoons (30ml) sriracha sauce
- Cooked rice, for serving
- Sesame seeds and chopped green onions, for garnish

Nutritional Information (Per Serving):
Calories 280 kcal
Proteins: 14 g
Fats: 15 g
Carbs: 24 g

DIRECTIONS

In a small bowl, mix together soy sauce, rice vinegar, sesame oil, and brown sugar. Set aside. Heat vegetable oil in a large skillet or wok over medium-high heat. Add cubed tofu and cook until golden brown and crispy on all sides, about 5-7 minutes. Remove tofu from the skillet and set aside. In the same skillet, add sliced onion and cook until translucent, about 2-3 minutes. Add minced garlic, sliced bell pepper, and snap peas. Cook for an additional 3-4 minutes, or until vegetables are tender-crisp. Return the cooked tofu to the skillet. Add grated ginger and sriracha sauce, stirring to combine all ingredients evenly. Cook for another 2-3 minutes to heat everything through. Pour the prepared sauce over the tofu and vegetables in the skillet. Stir well to coat everything in the sauce. Cook for another 1-2 minutes, or until the sauce thickens slightly. Serve the spicy tofu stir-fry hot over cooked rice. Garnish with sesame seeds and chopped green onions before serving.
Enjoy your delicious and spicy tofu stir-fry!

77. Eggplant Parmesan

Yield: 4 servings   Cooking time: 45 min

INGREDIENTS

- 2 medium eggplants, sliced into 1/4-inch rounds (about 600g)
- Salt
- 1 cup (120g) whole wheat bread crumbs
- 1/2 cup (50g) grated Parmesan cheese
- 2 eggs, beaten
- 2 cups (480ml) marinara sauce
- 1 cup (120g) shredded mozzarella cheese
- Fresh basil leaves for garnish

Nutritional Information (Per Serving):
Calories: 280 kcal
Proteins: 15 g
Fats: 10 g
Carbs: 30 g

DIRECTIONS

Preheat oven to 400°F (200°C) and line a baking sheet with parchment paper.
Salt eggplant slices and let sit in a colander for 20 minutes to remove excess moisture. Rinse and pat dry.
In a shallow bowl, mix bread crumbs and Parmesan cheese.
Dip eggplant slices in beaten eggs, then coat with bread crumb mixture.
Arrange breaded eggplant slices on the prepared baking sheet and bake for 20-25 minutes until golden brown and crispy.
Spread thin layer of marinara sauce in baking dish. Layer half of the baked eggplant slices, sauce, and shredded mozzarella. Repeat with remaining ingredients.
Bake for 15-20 minutes until cheese is melted and bubbly.
Let cool for a few minutes, garnish with fresh basil, and serve. Enjoy Eggplant Parmesan!

78. Vegan Stuffed Bell Peppers

Yield: 4 servings   Cooking time: 45 min

INGREDIENTS

4 large bell peppers
1 cup (185g) cooked quinoa
1 can (15 oz) black beans, drained and rinsed
1 cup (150g) corn kernels
1 cup (150g) diced tomatoes
1/2 cup (75g) diced onion
2 cloves garlic, minced
1 teaspoon ground cumin
1 teaspoon chili powder
Salt and pepper to taste
1/2 cup (60g) shredded vegan cheese
Fresh cilantro for garnish

Nutritional Information
(Per Serving):
Calories 320 kcal
Proteins: 12 g
Fats: 4 g
Carbs: 62 g

DIRECTIONS

Preheat the oven to 375°F (190°C). Cut the tops off the bell peppers and remove the seeds and membranes. Place the peppers upright in a baking dish. In a large mixing bowl, combine the cooked quinoa, black beans, corn, diced tomatoes, diced onion, minced garlic, ground cumin, chili powder, salt, and pepper. Mix well to combine. Spoon the quinoa and vegetable mixture into each bell pepper until they are filled to the top. Sprinkle shredded vegan cheese over the tops of the stuffed peppers. Cover the baking dish with aluminum foil and bake in the preheated oven for 25-30 minutes, or until the peppers are tender. Remove the foil and bake for an additional 5 minutes to melt the cheese and brown the tops of the peppers slightly. Remove from the oven and let cool for a few minutes before serving. Garnish with fresh cilantro before serving.
Enjoy these delicious and nutritious vegan stuffed bell peppers!

79. Cauliflower Fried Rice

Yield: 4 servings   Cooking time: 20 min

INGREDIENTS

1 large head cauliflower, grated (about 600g)
2 tbsp sesame oil
1 cup mixed vegetables (peas, carrots, bell peppers, corn)
2 cloves garlic, minced, 2 green onions, chopped
2 tbsp low-sodium soy sauce
1 tbsp rice vinegar
1 tsp sriracha sauce (optional)
Salt and pepper to taste
2 eggs, beaten
Sesame seeds and chopped fresh cilantro for garnish

Nutritional Information
(Per Serving):
Calories: 150 kcal
Proteins: 7 g
Fats: 7 g
Carbs: 18 g

DIRECTIONS

Heat 1 tbsp sesame oil in a large skillet. Stir-fry mixed vegetables and garlic until tender. Push to one side.
Scramble eggs on the empty side, then mix with vegetables. Remove from skillet.
Add remaining sesame oil to skillet. Stir-fry cauliflower until softened.
Return vegetable-egg mixture to skillet. Stir in green onions, soy sauce, rice vinegar, and sriracha. Season with salt and pepper.
Cook for 2-3 minutes until heated through. Garnish with sesame seeds and cilantro.
Serve and enjoy!

80. Black Bean and Sweet Potato Tacos

Yield: 4 servings　　　Cooking time: 25 min

INGREDIENTS

1 large sweet potato, peeled and diced (400g)
1 tbsp olive oil
1 tsp chili powder
1/2 tsp ground cumin
1/2 tsp paprika
Salt and pepper to taste
1 can (400g) black beans, drained and rinsed
1/2 cup diced red onion (about 75g)
1/4 cup chopped fresh cilantro
Juice of 1 lime
8 small corn tortillas
Optional toppings: diced avocado, shredded lettuce, salsa, Greek yogurt or sour cream

Nutritional Information (Per Serving):
Calories: 280 kcal
Proteins: 9 g
Fats: 4 g
Carbs: 53 g

DIRECTIONS

Preheat the oven to 400°F (200°C). Line a baking sheet with parchment paper.

In a mixing bowl, toss the diced sweet potato with olive oil, chili powder, cumin, paprika, salt, and pepper until evenly coated. Spread the seasoned sweet potatoes in a single layer on the prepared baking sheet. Roast in the preheated oven for 20-25 minutes, or until tender and lightly browned, stirring halfway through. In a separate mixing bowl, combine the black beans, diced red onion, chopped cilantro, and lime juice. Stir well to combine.

Warm the corn tortillas in a dry skillet or microwave according to package instructions.

To assemble the tacos, spoon some of the roasted sweet potatoes and black bean mixture onto each warmed tortilla. Add any desired toppings such as diced avocado, shredded lettuce, salsa, or Greek yogurt.

Serve immediately and enjoy these delicious and nutritious black bean and sweet potato tacos!

81. Vegan Pad Thai

Yield: 4 servings　　　Cooking time: 25 min

INGREDIENTS

200g rice noodles
2 tbsp sesame oil
2 cloves garlic, minced
1 red bell pepper, thinly sliced
1 carrot, julienned
1 cup broccoli florets, 1 cup bean sprouts
1/2 cup chopped green onions
1/4 cup chopped peanuts, Lime wedges
For the sauce:
1/4 cup soy sauce, 2 tbsp maple syrup
2 tbsp rice vinegar, 1 tbsp lime juice
1 tbsp sriracha sauce (adjust to taste)
1 tsp grated ginger
1 clove garlic, minced

Nutritional Information (Per Serving):
Calories: 320 kcal
Proteins: 10 g
Fats: 8 g
Carbs: 53 g

DIRECTIONS

Cook the rice noodles according to package instructions. Drain and set aside.

In a small bowl, whisk together all the sauce ingredients until well combined. Set aside.

Heat the sesame oil in a large skillet or wok over medium heat. Add the minced garlic and cook for 1 minute until fragrant.

Add the sliced bell pepper, julienned carrot, and broccoli florets to the skillet. Stir-fry for 3-4 minutes until the vegetables are tender-crisp.

Add the cooked rice noodles, bean sprouts, and chopped green onions to the skillet. Pour the sauce over the noodles and vegetables. Toss everything together until well combined and heated through.

Divide the vegan pad Thai among serving plates. Sprinkle with chopped peanuts and serve with lime wedges on the side.

Enjoy your delicious and flavorful vegan pad Thai!

82. Roasted Vegetable Quinoa Bowl

Yield: 4 servings Cooking time: 25 min

INGREDIENTS

Ingredients:
1 cup (185g) quinoa
2 cups (480ml) vegetable broth
2 cups (200g) broccoli florets
2 cups (200g) cauliflower florets
1 red bell pepper, sliced
1 yellow bell pepper, sliced
1 small red onion, sliced
2 tbsp (30ml) olive oil
2 cloves garlic, minced
1 tsp dried thyme
Salt and pepper to taste
1/4 cup (15g) chopped fresh parsley or cilantro
Lemon wedges, for serving

Nutritional Information (Per Serving):
Calories 280 kcal
Proteins: 9 g
Fats: 8 g
Carbs: 45 g

DIRECTIONS

Preheat the oven to 400°F (200°C). Rinse the quinoa under cold water. In a saucepan, combine the quinoa and vegetable broth. Bring to a boil, then reduce the heat, cover, and simmer for 15-20 minutes until the quinoa is tender and the liquid is absorbed. Fluff with a fork and set aside.

In a large mixing bowl, toss the broccoli florets, cauliflower florets, sliced bell peppers, and red onion with olive oil, minced garlic, dried thyme, salt, and pepper until well coated. Spread the seasoned vegetables in a single layer on a baking sheet lined with parchment paper. Roast in the preheated oven for 20-25 minutes, stirring halfway through, until the vegetables are tender and lightly browned.

Divide the cooked quinoa among serving bowls. Top with the roasted vegetables. Sprinkle with chopped fresh parsley or cilantro. Serve the roasted vegetable quinoa bowls with lemon wedges on the side for squeezing over the dish.

Enjoy this hearty and nutritious meal!

83. Zucchini Noodles with Vegan Pesto

Yield: 4 servings Cooking time: 20 min

INGREDIENTS

4 medium zucchinis, spiralized (about 600g)
1 cup (40g) fresh basil leaves
1/4 cup (30g) pine nuts
2 cloves garlic
2 tbsp (30ml) lemon juice
1/4 cup (60ml) extra virgin olive oil
Salt and pepper to taste
Vegan Parmesan cheese (optional, for serving)
Cherry tomatoes, halved (optional, for garnish)

Nutritional Information (Per Serving):
Calories: 320 kcal
Proteins: 10 g
Fats: 8 g
Carbs: 53 g

DIRECTIONS

Prepare the zucchini noodles using a spiralizer and set aside. In a food processor, combine the basil leaves, pine nuts, garlic, and lemon juice. Pulse until the ingredients are roughly chopped.

With the food processor running, slowly drizzle in the olive oil until the mixture forms a smooth pesto sauce. Season with salt and pepper to taste.

Heat a large skillet over medium heat. Add the zucchini noodles and cook for 2-3 minutes, tossing occasionally, until they are just tender.

Remove the skillet from the heat and add the vegan pesto sauce to the zucchini noodles. Toss until the noodles are evenly coated with the sauce.

Divide the zucchini noodles with vegan pesto among serving plates.

If desired, sprinkle with vegan Parmesan cheese and garnish with cherry tomatoes.

Serve immediately and enjoy this light and flavorful dish!

84. Portobello Mushroom Burgers

Yield: 4 servings Cooking time: 30 min

INGREDIENTS

Ingredients:
- 4 large portobello mushrooms
- 4 whole grain burger buns
- 2 tablespoons (30ml) balsamic vinegar
- 2 tablespoons (30ml) soy sauce
- 2 cloves garlic, minced
- 2 tablespoons (30ml) olive oil
- Salt and pepper to taste
- 1 large red onion, sliced
- 1 large tomato, sliced
- 2 cups (60g) fresh spinach leaves
- 1 avocado, sliced
- Optional toppings: sliced cheese, mustard, ketchup, pickles

Nutritional Information (Per Serving):
Calories 280 kcal
Proteins: 9 g
Fats: 8 g
Carbs: 45 g

DIRECTIONS

Clean the portobello mushrooms by wiping them with a damp paper towel. Remove the stems and discard. In a small bowl, whisk together balsamic vinegar, soy sauce, minced garlic, olive oil, salt, and pepper to make the marinade. Place the portobello mushrooms in a shallow dish and pour the marinade over them. Let them marinate for at least 15 minutes, flipping them halfway through to ensure even coating. Heat a grill pan or outdoor grill over medium heat. Place the marinated mushrooms on the grill and cook for about 5-7 minutes on each side, or until tender, brushing with any remaining marinade as they cook. While the mushrooms are grilling, toast the burger buns lightly on the grill or in a toaster. Assemble the burgers by placing a grilled portobello mushroom on the bottom half of each bun. Top with sliced onion, tomato, spinach leaves, avocado slices, and any other desired toppings. Cover with the top half of the burger bun and serve immediately. Enjoy your delicious and satisfying portobello mushroom burgers!

85. Vegan Creamy Mushroom Risotto

Yield: 4 servings Cooking time: 40 min

INGREDIENTS

- 1 ½ cups (300g) Arborio rice
- 4 cups (960ml) vegetable broth
- 2 tablespoons (30ml) olive oil
- 1 onion, finely chopped
- 2 cloves garlic, minced
- 10 oz (300g) mixed mushrooms (such as cremini, shiitake, and oyster), sliced
- ½ cup (120ml) white wine (optional)
- 1 teaspoon dried thyme
- Salt and pepper to taste
- ½ cup (120ml) unsweetened coconut milk
- ½ cup (30g) nutritional yeast (optional)
- Fresh parsley, chopped, for garnish (optional)

Nutritional Information (Per Serving):
Calories: 350 kcal
Proteins: 7 g
Fats: 8 g
Carbs: 58 g

DIRECTIONS

Heat vegetable broth in a saucepan over low heat and keep warm.
In a large skillet, sauté onion and garlic in olive oil over medium heat until softened, about 3-4 minutes.
Add mushrooms and cook until they release moisture and start to brown, about 5-7 minutes.
Stir in Arborio rice and cook for 1-2 minutes until well coated with oil and slightly translucent.
Pour in white wine, if using, and cook until absorbed. Gradually add warm vegetable broth, one ladleful at a time, stirring constantly until rice is creamy and tender, about 20-25 minutes.
Stir in dried thyme, salt, and pepper.
Reduce heat to low and stir in unsweetened coconut milk and nutritional yeast, if using, until creamy.
Remove from heat and let rest for a few minutes.
Garnish with fresh parsley, if desired, and serve hot. Enjoy vegan creamy mushroom risotto!

86. Chickpea and Vegetable Curry

Yield: 4 servings Cooking time: 40 min

INGREDIENTS

- 2 tablespoons (30ml) olive oil
- 1 onion, finely chopped
- 3 cloves garlic, minced
- 1 tablespoon (15g) grated ginger
- 1 red bell pepper, diced
- 1 yellow bell pepper, diced
- 1 zucchini, diced
- 1 cup (240ml) vegetable broth
- 1 can (15 oz/425g) chickpeas, drained and rinsed
- 1 can (14 oz/400ml) coconut milk
- 2 tablespoons (30g) curry powder
- 1 teaspoon (5g) ground turmeric
- 1 teaspoon (5g) ground cumin
- Salt and pepper to taste
- Cooked rice or naan bread, for serving
- Fresh cilantro leaves, for garnish

DIRECTIONS

Heat olive oil in a large skillet over medium heat. Add chopped onion and cook until softened, about 5 minutes.

Stir in minced garlic and grated ginger, cooking for another 1-2 minutes until fragrant.

Add diced bell peppers and zucchini to the skillet, cooking until slightly tender, about 5-7 minutes.

Pour in vegetable broth, then add drained chickpeas and coconut milk. Stir in curry powder, turmeric, and cumin. Season with salt and pepper to taste.

Simmer the curry over medium-low heat for 15-20 minutes, allowing flavors to meld and vegetables to become tender.

Serve the chickpea and vegetable curry over cooked rice or with naan bread. Garnish with fresh cilantro leaves before serving.

Enjoy your delicious and nutritious Chickpea and Vegetable Curry!

Nutritional Information (Per Serving):
Calories 340 kcal
Proteins: 9 g
Fats: 20 g
Carbs: 32 g

87. Sweet Potato and Chickpea Buddha Bowl

Yield: 4 servings Cooking time: 45 min

INGREDIENTS

- 2 large sweet potatoes, peeled and cubed (about 600g)
- 1 can (15 oz or 425g) chickpeas, drained and rinsed
- 2 tbsp (30ml) olive oil
- 1 tsp ground cumin
- 1 tsp smoked paprika
- Salt and pepper to taste
- 4 cups (120g) mixed greens (such as spinach, kale, or arugula)
- 1 avocado, sliced
- 1 cup (150g) cherry tomatoes, halved
- 1/4 cup (30g) pumpkin seeds
- 1/4 cup (60ml) tahini
- 2 tbsp (30ml) lemon juice
- 2 cloves garlic, minced
- 2 tbsp (30ml) water, or as needed
- Salt and pepper to taste

Nutritional Information (Per Serving):
Calories 425 kcal
Proteins: 12 g
Fats: 25 g
Carbs: 49 g

DIRECTIONS

Preheat the oven to 400°F (200°C). Line a baking sheet with parchment paper.

In a large bowl, toss the cubed sweet potatoes and chickpeas with olive oil, ground cumin, smoked paprika, salt, and pepper until evenly coated.

Spread the sweet potatoes and chickpeas in a single layer on the prepared baking sheet. Roast in the preheated oven for 25-30 minutes, or until the sweet potatoes are tender and golden brown.

While the sweet potatoes and chickpeas are roasting, prepare the tahini dressing. In a small bowl, whisk together tahini, lemon juice, minced garlic, water, salt, and pepper until smooth and creamy. Add more water as needed to reach your desired consistency.

To assemble the Buddha bowls, divide the mixed greens among four bowls. Top each bowl with roasted sweet potatoes and chickpeas, sliced avocado, cherry tomatoes, and pumpkin seeds.

Drizzle the tahini dressing over the Buddha bowls just before serving. Enjoy your nutritious and flavorful sweet potato and chickpea Buddha bowls!

Chapter 7: Keto-Friendly Recipes

Welcome to our Keto-Friendly Recipes chapter! Discover a world of delicious dishes crafted to support your low-carb lifestyle. From savory mains to indulgent desserts, each recipe offers a flavorful twist on classic favorites while keeping carbs in check. Whether you're a keto newbie or a seasoned pro, these dishes will satisfy your cravings and keep you on track with your dietary goals. Let's dive into the world of keto-friendly cooking and enjoy every flavorful bite!

88. Keto Lemon Garlic Butter Salmon

Yield: 4 servings   Cooking time: 25 min

INGREDIENTS

4 salmon fillets (about 170 grams each)
4 tablespoons unsalted butter (about 56 grams)
4 cloves garlic, minced
2 tablespoons fresh lemon juice (about 30 milliliters)
Zest of 1 lemon
1 teaspoon dried thyme
Salt and pepper to taste
Fresh parsley, chopped, for garnish

Nutritional Information (Per Serving):
Calories: 330 kcal
Proteins: 34 g
Fats: 20g
Carbs: 2 g

DIRECTIONS

Preheat your oven to 375°F (190°C). Line a baking sheet with parchment paper or aluminum foil.
Place the salmon fillets on the prepared baking sheet, skin side down. Season each fillet with salt and pepper to taste.
In a small saucepan, melt the butter over medium heat. Add the minced garlic and cook for 1-2 minutes until fragrant. Stir in the lemon juice, lemon zest, and dried thyme. Cook for another minute, then remove from heat.
Spoon the lemon garlic butter mixture evenly over each salmon fillet.
Bake in the preheated oven for 12-15 minutes, or until the salmon is cooked through and flakes easily with a fork.
Once cooked, remove the salmon from the oven and garnish with chopped fresh parsley.
Serve the keto lemon garlic butter salmon hot, accompanied by your favorite low-carb vegetables or salad.
Enjoy your delicious and nutritious meal!

89. Portobello Mushroom Burgers

Yield: 4 servings   Cooking time: 40 min

INGREDIENTS

1 medium cauliflower, riced (600g)
1 large egg
1/2 cup grated Parmesan cheese (50g)
1 tsp dried oregano
1/2 tsp garlic powder
Salt and pepper to taste
1/4 cup sugar-free marinara sauce (60ml)
1 cup cooked chicken breast, shredded (150g)
1/4 cup pesto sauce (60ml)
1 cup shredded mozzarella cheese (100g)
Fresh basil leaves, for garnish

DIRECTIONS

Preheat oven to 400°F (200°C). Line baking sheet with parchment paper.

Microwave cauliflower rice for 5-6 minutes, then squeeze out moisture.

Mix cauliflower with egg, Parmesan, oregano, garlic powder, salt, and pepper.

Spread cauliflower mixture onto baking sheet, bake 20-25 minutes until golden.

Top crust with marinara sauce, chicken, dollops of pesto, and mozzarella.

Bake for 10-12 minutes until cheese melts.

Garnish with fresh basil. Serve and enjoy!

Nutritional Information (Per Serving):
Calories: 250 kcal
Proteins: 20 g
Fats: 14 g
Carbs: 8 g

90. Keto Avocado Bacon Egg Cups

Yield: 4 servings   Cooking time: 25 min

INGREDIENTS

2 ripe avocados (about 300g)
4 slices bacon (about 100g)
4 large eggs
Salt and pepper to taste
Chopped fresh chives, for garnish

DIRECTIONS

Preheat oven to 400°F (200°C). Grease muffin tin.

Cut avocados in half, remove pits, and scoop out some flesh to create larger holes.

Wrap each avocado half with about 1 slice of bacon, placing it around the edges of the hole.

Crack an egg into each avocado half.

Season with salt and pepper.

Bake for 15-20 minutes until egg whites are set.

Garnish with chopped chives. Serve hot.

Nutritional Information (Per Serving):
Calories: 250 kcal
Proteins: 11 g
Fats: 21 g
Carbs: 7 g

91. Keto Zucchini Noodles with Creamy Alfredo Sauce

Yield: 4 servings   Cooking time: 40 min

INGREDIENTS
4 medium zucchinis (about 800g)
2 tablespoons butter (30g)
2 cloves garlic, minced
1 cup heavy cream (240ml)
1 cup grated Parmesan cheese (100g)
Salt and pepper to taste
Chopped fresh parsley, for garnish

Nutritional Information (Per Serving):
Calories 320 kcal
Proteins: 10 g
Fats: 27 g
Carbs: 8 g

DIRECTIONS
Spiralize zucchinis into noodles using a spiralizer.
In a large skillet, melt butter over medium heat. Add minced garlic and sauté for 1-2 minutes until fragrant.
Pour in heavy cream and bring to a simmer. Let it cook for about 5 minutes, stirring occasionally, until slightly thickened.
Gradually stir in grated Parmesan cheese until melted and smooth.
Season the sauce with salt and pepper to taste.
Add zucchini noodles to the skillet and toss with the creamy Alfredo sauce until well coated.
Cook for 3-4 minutes, stirring occasionally, until zucchini noodles are heated through but still crisp-tender.
Serve immediately, garnished with chopped fresh parsley.

92. Keto Chicken and Vegetable Stir-Fry

Yield: 4 servings   Cooking time: 25 min

INGREDIENTS
2 tablespoons avocado oil (30ml)
2 boneless, skinless chicken breasts, thinly sliced (about 400g)
2 cloves garlic, minced
1 inch ginger, grated
1 medium bell pepper, thinly sliced
1 cup broccoli florets (100g)
1 cup sliced mushrooms (100g)
1 medium zucchini, sliced (about 200g)
2 tablespoons soy sauce or tamari (30ml)
1 tablespoon sesame oil (15ml)
Salt and pepper to taste
Sesame seeds and chopped green onions, for garnish

Nutritional Information (Per Serving):
Calories: 280 kcal
Proteins: 25 g
Fats: 14 g
Carbs: 9 g

DIRECTIONS
Heat avocado oil in a large skillet or wok over medium-high heat. Add sliced chicken breasts to the skillet and cook until browned and cooked through, about 5-7 minutes.
Remove chicken from skillet and set aside. In the same skillet, add minced garlic and grated ginger. Sauté for 1-2 minutes until fragrant. Add sliced bell pepper, broccoli florets, mushrooms, and sliced zucchini to the skillet. Cook for 5-7 minutes, stirring occasionally, until vegetables are tender-crisp. Return cooked chicken to the skillet with the vegetables. Drizzle soy sauce or tamari and sesame oil over the chicken and vegetables. Toss until everything is evenly coated. Season with salt and pepper to taste.
Cook for another 2-3 minutes until everything is heated through.
Serve hot, garnished with sesame seeds and chopped green onions.

93. Grilled Steak with Garlic Butter

Yield: 4 servings   Cooking time: 30 min

INGREDIENTS

- 4 beef steaks (such as ribeye, sirloin, or fillet), about 6 oz each (170g)
- Salt and black pepper, to taste
- 2 tablespoons olive oil (30ml)
- 4 cloves garlic, minced
- 4 tablespoons unsalted butter (60g)
- 2 tablespoons chopped fresh parsley (optional)
- Lemon wedges, for serving

DIRECTIONS

Preheat grill to high heat. Season the steaks generously with salt and black pepper on both sides. Drizzle olive oil over the steaks and rub to coat evenly. Place the steaks on the hot grill and cook for about 4-5 minutes per side for medium-rare, or until desired doneness is reached.

While the steaks are grilling, prepare the garlic butter. In a small saucepan, melt the butter over medium heat.

Add the minced garlic to the melted butter and cook for 1-2 minutes until fragrant. Remove the garlic butter from heat and stir in chopped parsley, if using.

Once the steaks are cooked to your liking, transfer them to a plate and let rest for a few minutes.

Serve the grilled steaks with a generous dollop of garlic butter on top. Garnish with lemon wedges and additional chopped parsley, if desired.

Enjoy your succulent grilled steak with garlic butter!

Nutritional Information (Per Serving):
Calories 400 kcal
Proteins: 32 g
Fats: 29 g
Carbs: 1 g

94. Coconut Curry Shrimp with Cauliflower Rice

Yield: 4 servings   Cooking time: 25 min

INGREDIENTS

- 1 lb (450g) large shrimp, peeled and deveined
- Salt and black pepper, to taste
- 2 tablespoons coconut oil (30ml)
- 1 small onion, finely chopped
- 3 cloves garlic, minced
- 1 tablespoon ginger, minced
- 2 tablespoons red curry paste
- 1 can (13.5 oz) coconut milk (400ml)
- 2 cups cauliflower rice (200g)
- Fresh cilantro, for garnish
- Lime wedges, for serving

DIRECTIONS

Season the shrimp with salt and black pepper to taste. In a large skillet, heat the coconut oil over medium heat. Add the chopped onion to the skillet and sauté for 2-3 minutes until translucent. Stir in the minced garlic and ginger, and cook for another minute until fragrant.

Add the red curry paste to the skillet and cook for 1-2 minutes, stirring constantly. Pour in the coconut milk and bring the mixture to a simmer. Add the seasoned shrimp to the skillet and cook for 4-5 minutes until the shrimp are pink and cooked through. While the shrimp is cooking, prepare the cauliflower rice according to package instructions, or make your own by pulsing cauliflower florets in a food processor until they resemble rice.

Serve the coconut curry shrimp over the cauliflower rice. Garnish with fresh cilantro and serve with lime wedges on the side.

Enjoy your flavorful and aromatic coconut curry shrimp with cauliflower rice!

Nutritional Information (Per Serving):
Calories: 250 kcal
Proteins: 11 g
Fats: 21 g
Carbs: 7 g

95. Bacon-Wrapped Asparagus Bundles

Yield: 4 servings   Cooking time: 35 min

INGREDIENTS

1 bunch asparagus spears (about 20 spears)
8 slices bacon
2 tablespoons olive oil (30ml)
Salt and black pepper, to taste
1 tablespoon balsamic glaze (15ml), for drizzling (optional)

DIRECTIONS

Preheat your oven to 400°F (200°C). Line a baking sheet with parchment paper or aluminum foil for easy cleanup.

Wash the asparagus spears and trim off the tough ends.

Divide the asparagus into bundles, wrapping each bundle with a slice of bacon. Secure the bacon in place with toothpicks if necessary. Place the bacon-wrapped asparagus bundles on the prepared baking sheet.

Drizzle the olive oil over the bundles and season with salt and black pepper to taste. Bake in the preheated oven for 12-15 minutes, or until the bacon is crispy and the asparagus is tender. Once cooked, remove the toothpicks from the bundles and transfer them to a serving platter.

Optionally, drizzle with balsamic glaze before serving for extra flavor.

Serve the bacon-wrapped asparagus bundles as a delicious and savory appetizer or side dish.

Enjoy!

Nutritional Information (Per Serving):
Calories: 210 kcal
Proteins: 8 g
Fats: 18 g
Carbs: 4 g

96. Eggplant Lasagna with Ricotta and Spinach

Yield: 6 servings   Cooking time: 75 min

INGREDIENTS

2 large eggplants, thinly sliced lengthwise
2 cups ricotta cheese (450g)
1 cup spinach, chopped (90g)
1 cup marinara sauce (240ml)
1 cup shredded mozzarella cheese (120g)
1/2 cup grated Parmesan cheese (50g)
2 cloves garlic, minced
1 tablespoon olive oil (15ml)
Salt and pepper, to taste
Fresh basil leaves, for garnish

DIRECTIONS

Preheat oven to 375°F (190°C). Grease a baking dish.

Cook minced garlic in olive oil until fragrant. Add spinach, cook until wilted.

In a bowl, mix ricotta cheese with cooked spinach. Season with salt and pepper.

Layer eggplant slices in the baking dish. Spread half of ricotta mixture over eggplant.

Pour half of marinara sauce over ricotta, then sprinkle half of mozzarella and Parmesan.

Repeat layers with remaining ingredients.

Cover with foil and bake for 30 minutes.

Remove foil and bake for additional 15 minutes until cheese is golden. Let cool for a few minutes, garnish with basil leaves, then serve.

Nutritional Information (Per Serving):
Calories: 250 kcal
Proteins: 11 g
Fats: 21 g
Carbs: 7 g

97. Turkey Avocado Lettuce Wraps

Yield: 4 servings   Cooking time: 35 min

INGREDIENTS
1 lb ground turkey (450g)
1 avocado, diced
1/2 cup diced tomatoes (75g)
1/4 cup diced red onion (40g)
1/4 cup chopped cilantro (15g)
2 tbsp lime juice (30ml)
Salt and pepper, to taste
8 large lettuce leaves

DIRECTIONS
In a skillet over medium heat, cook ground turkey until browned and cooked through. Season with salt and pepper.
In a bowl, mix together diced avocado, tomatoes, red onion, cilantro, and lime juice to make salsa.
Place a spoonful of cooked turkey onto each lettuce leaf.
Top with avocado salsa.
Roll up the lettuce leaves to form wraps.
Serve immediately.

Nutritional Information (Per Serving):
Calories 230 kcal
Proteins: 20 g
Fats: 12 g
Carbs: 9 g

98. Low-Carb Taco Stuffed Peppers

Yield: 4 servings   Cooking time: 45 min

INGREDIENTS
4 bell peppers, halved and seeds removed
1 lb ground beef (450g)
1 packet taco seasoning
1 cup diced tomatoes (150g)
1/2 cup shredded cheddar cheese (60g)
1/4 cup chopped cilantro (15g)
Sour cream, for topping (optional)
Sliced green onions, for garnish (optional

DIRECTIONS
Preheat oven to 375°F (190°C).
In a skillet over medium heat, cook ground beef until browned. Drain excess fat.
Stir in taco seasoning and diced tomatoes. Cook for 5 minutes.
Place bell pepper halves in a baking dish.
Spoon taco meat mixture into each bell pepper half.
Cover with foil and bake for 25 minutes.
Remove foil, sprinkle shredded cheese over the tops, and bake for an additional 5 minutes until cheese is melted and bubbly.
Garnish with chopped cilantro, sour cream, and sliced green onions if desired.
Serve hot.

Nutritional Information (Per Serving):
Calories: 330 kcal
Proteins: 25 g
Fats: 20 g
Carbs: 12 g

99. Spinach and Feta Stuffed Chicken Breasts

Yield: 4 servings   Cooking time: 35 min

INGREDIENTS
- 4 boneless, skinless chicken breasts
- 2 cups chopped spinach (60g)
- 1/2 cup crumbled feta cheese (75g)
- 2 cloves garlic, minced
- 1 tbsp olive oil (15ml)
- Salt and pepper, to taste
- Toothpicks

DIRECTIONS
Preheat oven to 375°F (190°C).
In a skillet over medium heat, heat olive oil. Add minced garlic and cook until fragrant.
Add chopped spinach to the skillet and cook until wilted.
Remove skillet from heat and stir in crumbled feta cheese.
Season chicken breasts with salt and pepper. Slice a pocket into the side of each chicken breast.
Stuff each chicken breast with spinach and feta mixture. Secure the openings with toothpicks.
Place stuffed chicken breasts in a baking dish.
Bake for 20-25 minutes until chicken is cooked through and juices run clear.
Remove toothpicks before serving.

Nutritional Information (Per Serving):
Calories: 280 kcal
Proteins: 35 g
Fats: 12 g
Carbs: 2 g

100. Keto Beef and Broccoli

Yield: 4 servings   Cooking time: 30 min

INGREDIENTS
- 450g flank steak, thinly sliced
- 60ml soy sauce or tamari
- 30ml olive oil
- 3 cloves garlic, minced
- 1 tsp ginger, minced
- 200g broccoli florets
- 1 tbsp sesame seeds, for garnish
- Salt and pepper, to taste

DIRECTIONS
In a bowl, marinate thinly sliced flank steak with soy sauce, minced garlic, minced ginger, salt, and pepper for 15-20 minutes.
Heat olive oil in a skillet over medium-high heat. Add marinated beef and cook until browned, about 2-3 minutes per side.
Remove beef from skillet and set aside.
In the same skillet, add broccoli florets and cook until tender, about 3-4 minutes.
Return cooked beef to the skillet and toss with broccoli until heated through.
Garnish with sesame seeds and serve hot.

Nutritional Information (Per Serving):
Calories: 280 kcal
Proteins: 25 g
Fats: 16 g
Carbs: 6 g

101. Creamy Garlic Parmesan Zoodles

Yield: 4 servings Cooking time: 20 min

INGREDIENTS
- 4 medium zucchini (about 800g), spiralized
- 30g butter
- 3 cloves garlic, minced
- 120ml heavy cream
- 25g grated Parmesan cheese
- Salt and pepper, to taste
- Chopped fresh parsley, for garnish

DIRECTIONS
In a skillet over medium heat, melt butter. Add minced garlic and cook until fragrant.
Add spiralized zucchini to the skillet and cook for 2-3 minutes until tender.
Pour heavy cream over the zucchini and stir until heated through.
Stir in grated Parmesan cheese until melted and creamy.
Season with salt and pepper to taste.
Garnish with chopped fresh parsley and serve hot.

Nutritional Information (Per Serving):
Calories 180 kcal
Proteins: 4 g
Fats: 14 g
Carbs: 8 g

102. Mediterranean Grilled Vegetable Salad

Yield: 4 servings Cooking time: 25 min

INGREDIENTS
- 2 zucchinis (about 400g), sliced lengthwise
- 2 bell peppers (red and yellow), quartered
- 1 red onion, sliced into rounds
- 150g cherry tomatoes, halved
- 50g Kalamata olives, pitted
- 30ml olive oil
- 30ml balsamic vinegar
- Salt and pepper, to taste
- Fresh basil leaves, for garnish

DIRECTIONS
Preheat grill to medium-high heat.
In a bowl, toss sliced zucchinis, bell peppers, and red onion with olive oil, balsamic vinegar, salt, and pepper.
Grill vegetables until tender and charred, about 4-5 minutes per side.
Remove grilled vegetables from the grill and let them cool slightly.
In a large bowl, combine grilled vegetables with cherry tomatoes and Kalamata olives.
Drizzle with extra olive oil and balsamic vinegar if desired.
Garnish with fresh basil leaves and serve warm or at room temperature.

Nutritional Information (Per Serving):
Calories: 120 kcal
Proteins: 2 g
Fats: 7 g
Carbs: 14 g

Chapter 8: Gluten-Free Delights

Welcome to our Gluten-Free Delights chapter! In this section, we celebrate the joy of gluten-free eating with a collection of mouthwatering recipes that cater to those with gluten sensitivities or dietary preferences. From hearty meals to sweet treats, each recipe has been carefully crafted to ensure both flavor and texture are not compromised. Whether you're gluten intolerant or simply exploring the world of gluten-free cuisine, you'll find plenty of inspiration here to create delicious and satisfying meals. Let's embark on a journey of culinary exploration and embrace the gluten-free lifestyle with delight!

103. Green Quinoa and Avocado Salad

Yield: 4 servings   Cooking time: 15 min

INGREDIENTS

1 cup cooked quinoa (185 grams)
1 ripe avocado, diced
1 small cucumber, diced (about 150 grams)
1 cup cherry tomatoes, halved (about 150 grams)
2 cups fresh spinach leaves
1/4 cup fresh cilantro, chopped (about 15 grams)
2 tablespoons green onions, chopped
Juice of 1 lime
2 tablespoons olive oil
Salt and pepper to taste

DIRECTIONS

In a large bowl, combine the cooked quinoa, diced avocado, cucumber, cherry tomatoes, spinach leaves, chopped cilantro, and green onions.

In a small bowl, whisk together the lime juice, olive oil, salt, and pepper to make the dressing.

Pour the dressing over the salad ingredients and toss gently to coat evenly.

Serve immediately or refrigerate for later.

Nutritional Information (Per Serving):
Calories: 220 kcal
Proteins: 5 g
Fats: 14g
Carbs: 22 g

104. Gluten-Free Oat Banana Pancakes

Yield: 4 servings   Cooking time: 15 min

INGREDIENTS

- 1 cup gluten-free rolled oats (90 grams)
- 2 ripe bananas
- 2 eggs
- 1/2 teaspoon ground cinnamon
- 1/2 teaspoon vanilla extract
- 1/4 teaspoon baking powder
- Pinch of salt
- Coconut oil or butter for cooking

DIRECTIONS

In a blender or food processor, blend the rolled oats until they form a fine flour-like consistency.

Add the ripe bananas, eggs, ground cinnamon, vanilla extract, baking powder, and a pinch of salt to the blender. Blend until smooth and well combined.

Heat a non-stick skillet or griddle over medium heat and lightly grease with coconut oil or butter.

Pour about 1/4 cup of the pancake batter onto the skillet for each pancake.

Cook for 2-3 minutes on one side, or until bubbles start to form on the surface of the pancake.

Flip the pancakes and cook for another 1-2 minutes on the other side, or until golden brown and cooked through.

Repeat with the remaining batter.

Serve the pancakes warm with your favorite toppings such as fresh fruit, maple syrup, or yogurt.

Nutritional Information (Per Serving):
Calories 150 kcal
Proteins: 5 g
Fats: 4 g
Carbs: 25 g

105. Mushroom Quinoa Patties with Green Peas

Yield: 4 servings   Cooking time: 25 min

INGREDIENTS

- 1 cup cooked quinoa (185 grams)
- 1 cup mushrooms, finely chopped (100 grams)
- 1/2 cup green peas, cooked and mashed (80 grams)
- 1/4 cup grated Parmesan cheese (25 grams)
- 2 cloves garlic, minced
- 1/4 cup finely chopped onion (40 grams)
- 1/4 cup chopped fresh parsley
- 1 egg
- 2 tablespoons almond flour (20 grams)
- Salt and pepper to taste
- Olive oil for cooking

DIRECTIONS

In a large mixing bowl, combine the cooked quinoa, chopped mushrooms, mashed green peas, grated Parmesan cheese, minced garlic, chopped onion, chopped parsley, egg, almond flour, salt, and pepper. Mix until well combined.

Heat a tablespoon of olive oil in a skillet over medium heat.

Form the quinoa mixture into patties using your hands.

Place the patties in the skillet and cook for 4-5 minutes on each side, or until golden brown and cooked through.

Remove the patties from the skillet and drain on paper towels to remove any excess oil.

Serve the mushroom quinoa patties warm as a delicious and nutritious gluten-free meal.

Nutritional Information (Per Serving):
Calories: 180 kcal
Proteins: 9 g
Fats: 6 g
Carbs: 22 g

106. Sesame Cauliflower with Teriyaki Sauce

Yield: 4 servings   Cooking time: 15 min

INGREDIENTS

1 head cauliflower, cut into florets (600 gr)
2 tablespoons sesame oil (30 ml)
2 tablespoons soy sauce (30 ml)
2 tablespoons rice vinegar (30 ml)
2 tablespoons honey or maple syrup (30 ml)
1 tablespoon minced ginger
2 cloves garlic, minced
1 tablespoon cornstarch (10 grams) mixed with
2 tablespoons water (30 ml)
2 tablespoons sesame seeds, for garnish
Chopped green onions, for garnish

Nutritional Information (Per Serving):
Calories 150 kcal
Proteins: 5 g
Fats: 4 g
Carbs: 25 g

DIRECTIONS

Preheat oven to 200°C (400°F) and line a baking sheet with parchment paper. Whisk sesame oil, soy sauce, rice vinegar, honey or maple syrup, minced ginger, and minced garlic in a small bowl for the teriyaki sauce.

Toss cauliflower florets in a large bowl with teriyaki sauce until evenly coated. Spread cauliflower on prepared baking sheet in a single layer. Roast in oven for 20-25 minutes until tender and caramelized. While cauliflower roasts, mix cornstarch with water to make a slurry. Transfer roasted cauliflower to a skillet or saucepan. Pour cornstarch slurry over cauliflower and cook over medium heat, stirring constantly, until sauce thickens (2-3 minutes).

Remove from heat and transfer sesame cauliflower to a serving dish.

Garnish with sesame seeds and chopped green onions.

Serve as a delicious gluten-free side dish or appetizer.

107. Caprese Salad with Red Quinoa

Yield: 4 servings   Cooking time: 15 min

INGREDIENTS

1 cup cooked red quinoa (185 grams)
2 cups cherry tomatoes, halved (300 grams)
1 cup fresh mozzarella balls, halved (125 grams)
1/4 cup fresh basil leaves, chopped (10 grams)
2 tablespoons balsamic glaze (30 ml)
Salt and pepper to taste

DIRECTIONS

In a large bowl, combine the cooked red quinoa, cherry tomatoes, fresh mozzarella balls, and chopped basil leaves.

Drizzle the balsamic glaze over the salad and toss gently to combine.

Season with salt and pepper to taste.

Serve immediately or refrigerate until ready to serve.

Nutritional Information (Per Serving):
Calories: 200 kcal
Proteins: 8 g
Fats: 10 g
Carbs: 20 g

108. Baked Sweet Potatoes with Walnuts and Cranberries

Yield: 4 servings   Cooking time: 70 min

INGREDIENTS

4 medium sweet potatoes (800 grams)
1/2 cup walnuts, chopped (60 grams)
1/4 cup dried cranberries (40 grams)
2 tablespoons maple syrup (30 ml)
1 tablespoon coconut oil, melted (15 ml)
1 teaspoon cinnamon
Salt to taste

Nutritional Information (Per Serving):
Calories 250 kcal
Proteins: 4 g
Fats: 10g
Carbs: 40 g

DIRECTIONS

Preheat the oven to 200°C (400°F) and line a baking sheet with parchment paper.

Scrub the sweet potatoes and pierce them with a fork in several places.

Place the sweet potatoes on the prepared baking sheet and bake for 45-60 minutes, or until tender.

In a small bowl, mix together the chopped walnuts, dried cranberries, maple syrup, melted coconut oil, cinnamon, and salt.

When the sweet potatoes are done, remove them from the oven and let them cool slightly.

Slice each sweet potato open lengthwise and fluff the flesh with a fork.

Spoon the walnut and cranberry mixture over the sweet potatoes.

Serve immediately as a delicious side dish or light meal.

109. Shrimp Coconut Milk Soup

Yield: 4 servings   Cooking time: 35 min

INGREDIENTS

1 tablespoon coconut oil
1 onion, diced
2 cloves garlic, minced
1 tablespoon ginger, grated
2 cups coconut milk (480 ml)
2 cups vegetable broth (480 ml)
1 red bell pepper, sliced
1 cup snap peas (150 grams)
1 pound shrimp, peeled and deveined (450 gr)
Juice of 1 lime
Salt and pepper to taste
Fresh cilantro, for garnish

Nutritional Information (Per Serving):
Calories: 300 kcal
Proteins: 25 g
Fats: 20 g
Carbs: 10 g

DIRECTIONS

In a large pot, heat the coconut oil over medium heat.

Add the diced onion, minced garlic, and grated ginger to the pot. Saute for 2-3 minutes, or until the onion is translucent and fragrant.

Pour in the coconut milk and vegetable broth, and bring the mixture to a simmer.

Add the sliced red bell pepper and snap peas to the pot. Cook for 5 minutes, or until the vegetables are tender.

Stir in the peeled and deveined shrimp and cook for an additional 3-4 minutes, or until the shrimp are pink and opaque.

Squeeze the lime juice into the soup and season with salt and pepper to taste.

Ladle the shrimp coconut milk soup into bowls and garnish with fresh cilantro.

Serve hot as a comforting and flavorful gluten-free meal.

110. Thai Shrimp Salad with Sesame Dressing

Yield: 4 servings   Cooking time: 20 min

INGREDIENTS

1 pound shrimp, peeled and deveined (450 g)
4 cups mixed salad greens (120 grams)
1 cucumber, thinly sliced (200 grams)
1 carrot, julienned (100 grams)
1/4 cup chopped fresh cilantro (10 grams)
1/4 cup chopped fresh mint leaves (10 grams)
2 tablespoons sesame seeds
1/4 cup lime juice (60 ml),
2 tablespoons fish sauce
1 tablespoon soy sauce (gluten-free if needed)
1 tablespoon honey, 1 tablespoon sesame oil
1 clove garlic, minced, 1 teaspoon grated ginger
Salt and pepper to taste

Nutritional Information
(Per Serving):
Calories 250 kcal
Proteins: 25 g
Fats: 10g
Carbs: 15 g

DIRECTIONS

In a large bowl, combine the salad greens, sliced cucumber, julienned carrot, chopped cilantro, and chopped mint leaves.

Heat a grill or grill pan over medium-high heat. Season the shrimp with salt and pepper, then grill for 2-3 minutes on each side until cooked through.

Add the grilled shrimp to the salad bowl.

In a small bowl, whisk together the lime juice, fish sauce, soy sauce, honey, sesame oil, minced garlic, and grated ginger to make the dressing.

Drizzle the dressing over the salad and toss gently to coat.

Sprinkle sesame seeds over the salad before serving.

Serve immediately as a refreshing and flavorful gluten-free meal.

111. Spinach Avocado Pesto with Gluten-Free Pasta

Yield: 4 servings   Cooking time: 20 min

INGREDIENTS

8 ounces gluten-free pasta (225 grams)
2 cups fresh spinach leaves (60 grams)
1 ripe avocado, peeled and pitted
1/4 cup fresh basil leaves (10 grams)
1/4 cup pine nuts (35 grams)
2 cloves garlic
Juice of 1 lemon
2 tablespoons olive oil
Salt and pepper to taste
Grated Parmesan cheese (optional, for serving)

Nutritional Information
(Per Serving):
Calories: 300 kcal
Proteins: 8 g
Fats: 15 g
Carbs: 35 g

DIRECTIONS

Cook the gluten-free pasta according to the package instructions. Drain and set aside.

In a food processor, combine the fresh spinach leaves, ripe avocado, fresh basil leaves, pine nuts, garlic cloves, lemon juice, olive oil, salt, and pepper.

Blend until smooth and creamy, adding more olive oil if necessary to reach the desired consistency.

Toss the cooked pasta with the spinach avocado pesto until well coated.

Serve the pasta with grated Parmesan cheese on top, if desired.

Enjoy your delicious and nutritious gluten-free meal!

112. Grilled Turmeric and Ginger Chicken

Yield: 4 servings   Cooking time: 25 min

INGREDIENTS

- 4 boneless, skinless chicken breasts
- 2 tablespoons olive oil
- 1 tablespoon turmeric powder
- 1 tablespoon grated ginger
- 2 cloves garlic, minced
- Juice of 1 lemon
- Salt and pepper to taste
- Fresh cilantro, for garnish

DIRECTIONS

In a bowl, whisk together the olive oil, turmeric powder, grated ginger, minced garlic, lemon juice, salt, and pepper to make the marinade.

Place the chicken breasts in a shallow dish and pour the marinade over them. Ensure the chicken is evenly coated.

Cover and refrigerate for at least 30 minutes, or up to 4 hours.

Preheat the grill to medium-high heat. Remove the chicken from the marinade and discard any excess marinade.

Grill the chicken breasts for 6-8 minutes on each side, or until cooked through and no longer pink in the center.

Transfer the grilled chicken to a serving platter and garnish with fresh cilantro.

Serve hot with your favorite side dishes for a delicious and healthy gluten-free meal.

Nutritional Information (Per Serving):
Calories 250 kcal
Proteins: 30g
Fats: 10g
Carbs: 5 g

113. Asparagus with Sautéed Mushrooms and Almonds

Yield: 4 servings   Cooking time: 20 min

INGREDIENTS

- 1 bunch asparagus, trimmed (200 grams)
- 2 cups sliced mushrooms (150 grams)
- 2 tablespoons olive oil
- 2 cloves garlic, minced
- Salt and pepper to taste
- 1/4 cup sliced almonds, toasted

DIRECTIONS

Heat the olive oil in a large skillet over medium heat. Add the minced garlic and sauté for 1 minute, or until fragrant.

Add the sliced mushrooms to the skillet and cook for 5-7 minutes, or until they are tender and golden brown.

While the mushrooms are cooking, bring a pot of water to a boil. Add the trimmed asparagus and blanch for 2-3 minutes, or until bright green and crisp-tender. Drain and set aside.

Season the mushrooms with salt and pepper to taste.

Arrange the blanched asparagus on a serving platter and top with the sautéed mushrooms.

Sprinkle the toasted sliced almonds over the top.

Serve the asparagus with sautéed mushrooms and almonds as a delicious and nutritious gluten-free side dish.

Nutritional Information (Per Serving):
Calories: 150 kcal
Proteins: 5 g
Fats: 5 g
Carbs: 10 g

114. Tuna Steak in Teriyaki Sauce with Quinoa

Yield: 4 servings   Cooking time: 25 min

INGREDIENTS

4 tuna steaks (4-6 ounces each)
1/4 cup gluten-free soy sauce
2 tablespoons honey or maple syrup
1 tablespoon rice vinegar
1 teaspoon grated ginger
2 cloves garlic, minced
2 cups cooked quinoa (350 grams)
2 green onions, thinly sliced
Sesame seeds, for garnish

Nutritional Information (Per Serving):
Calories 250 kcal
Proteins: 30g
Fats: 10g
Carbs: 5 g

DIRECTIONS

In a small bowl, whisk together the gluten-free soy sauce, honey or maple syrup, rice vinegar, grated ginger, and minced garlic to make the teriyaki sauce.

Place the tuna steaks in a shallow dish and pour half of the teriyaki sauce over them. Reserve the remaining sauce for later. Marinate the tuna steaks for 15-30 minutes, turning occasionally to coat. Heat a grill or grill pan over medium-high heat. Remove the tuna steaks from the marinade and discard any excess marinade. Grill the tuna steaks for 2-3 minutes on each side, or until they reach your desired level of doneness. While the tuna is grilling, reheat the remaining teriyaki sauce in a small saucepan over medium heat until warmed through. Serve the grilled tuna steaks over cooked quinoa, drizzle with the warmed teriyaki sauce, and garnish with thinly sliced green onions and sesame seeds.

Enjoy your gluten-free tuna steak in teriyaki sauce with quinoa as a flavorful and protein-packed meal!

115. Creamy Broccoli Almond Soup

Yield: 4 servings   Cooking time: 40 min

INGREDIENTS

2 tablespoons olive oil
1 onion, chopped
2 cloves garlic, minced
4 cups chopped broccoli florets (350 grams)
4 cups vegetable broth (960 ml)
1/2 cup almond butter (120 grams)
Salt and pepper to taste
Sliced almonds, for garnish
Fresh parsley, for garnish

Nutritional Information (Per Serving):
Calories: 250 kcal
Proteins: 8 g
Fats: 20 g
Carbs: 15 g

DIRECTIONS

In a large pot, heat the olive oil over medium heat. Add the chopped onion and minced garlic, and sauté until softened and fragrant, about 5 minutes.

Add the chopped broccoli florets to the pot and sauté for another 2-3 minutes.

Pour in the vegetable broth and bring the mixture to a boil. Reduce the heat to low, cover, and simmer for 15-20 minutes, or until the broccoli is tender.

Using an immersion blender, blend the soup until smooth and creamy.

Stir in the almond butter until well incorporated into the soup.

Season with salt and pepper to taste.

Ladle the creamy broccoli almond soup into bowls and garnish with sliced almonds and fresh parsley before serving.

Chapter 9: Dairy-Free Options

Welcome to the "Dairy-Free Options" chapter! Explore a variety of delicious recipes free of dairy products. From creamy soups to decadent desserts, enjoy dairy-free alternatives packed with wholesome ingredients. Say goodbye to dairy without sacrificing taste or texture. Let's dive in and discover the wonderful world of dairy-free cooking together!

116. Vegan Cauliflower Mac and Cheese

Yield: 4 servings Cooking time: 30 min

INGREDIENTS

1 head cauliflower, cut into florets (500 g)
2 cups cooked macaroni or pasta of choice (240 g)
1 cup cashews, soaked in water for 2 hours, drained (150 g)
1/2 cup nutritional yeast (30 g)
1/4 cup almond milk (60 ml)
2 tablespoons lemon juice (30 ml)
2 cloves garlic, minced
1 teaspoon Dijon mustard (5 ml)
Salt and pepper to taste
Chopped parsley for garnish (optional)

Nutritional Information (Per Serving):
Calories : 250 kcal
Proteins: 12 g
Fats: 10 g
Carbs: 30 g

DIRECTIONS

Preheat the oven to 375°F (190°C). Lightly grease a baking dish. Steam or boil the cauliflower florets until tender, about 8-10 minutes. Drain and set aside.

In a blender, combine the soaked cashews, nutritional yeast, almond milk, lemon juice, minced garlic, Dijon mustard, salt, and pepper. Blend until smooth and creamy.

In a large bowl, mix together the cooked macaroni and steamed cauliflower. Pour the cashew cheese sauce over the macaroni and cauliflower mixture. Stir until everything is well coated.

Transfer the mixture to the prepared baking dish and spread it out evenly. Bake in the preheated oven for 20-25 minutes, or until bubbly and lightly golden on top.

Remove from the oven and let it cool for a few minutes before serving.

Garnish with chopped parsley if desired, and serve this delicious vegan cauliflower mac and cheese hot.

117. Almond Milk Smoothie Bowl with Mixed Fruits

Yield: 2 servings   Cooking time: 10 min

INGREDIENTS
- 2 cups mixed fruits (such as berries, banana, mango) (300 g)
- 1 cup almond milk (240 ml)
- 1 tablespoon chia seeds (15 g)
- 2 tablespoons almond butter (30 g)
- 1 tablespoon honey or maple syrup (15 ml)
- Toppings: sliced almonds, shredded coconut, fresh fruits

DIRECTIONS
In a blender, combine the mixed fruits, almond milk, chia seeds, almond butter, and honey (or maple syrup). Blend until smooth and creamy.

Pour the smoothie into bowls.

Top with sliced almonds, shredded coconut, and additional fresh fruits.

Serve immediately and enjoy this nutritious almond milk smoothie bowl with mixed fruits!

Nutritional Information (Per Serving):
Calories 200 kcal
Proteins: 5g
Fats: 10g
Carbs: 30 g

---

118. Dairy-Free Vegetable Curry with Quinoa

Yield: 4 servings   Cooking time: 30 min

INGREDIENTS
- 1 cup quinoa, rinsed (185 g)
- 2 cups water (480 ml)
- 2 tablespoons coconut oil (30 ml)
- 1 onion, chopped
- 3 cloves garlic, minced
- 1 tablespoon grated ginger (15 g)
- 2 carrots, diced (150 g)
- 2 cups cauliflower florets (250 g)
- 1 cup green beans, trimmed and halved (150 g)
- 1 can (14 oz) coconut milk (400 ml)
- 2 tablespoons red curry paste (30 g)
- Salt and pepper to taste
- Fresh cilantro for garnish (optional)

DIRECTIONS
In a saucepan, combine the quinoa and water. Bring to a boil, then reduce the heat to low, cover, and simmer for 15-20 minutes, or until the quinoa is cooked and fluffy. Remove from heat and set aside. In a large skillet, heat the coconut oil over medium heat. Add the chopped onion and cook until softened, about 3-4 minutes. Stir in the minced garlic and grated ginger, and cook for an additional 1-2 minutes. Add the diced carrots, cauliflower florets, and green beans to the skillet. Cook for 5-7 minutes, or until the vegetables are tender. Stir in the coconut milk and red curry paste. Simmer for another 5 minutes, allowing the flavors to meld together. Season with salt and pepper to taste.

Serve the vegetable curry over cooked quinoa, garnished with fresh cilantro if desired.

Enjoy this dairy-free vegetable curry with quinoa as a delicious and nutritious meal!

Nutritional Information (Per Serving):
Calories: 300 kcal
Proteins: 8 g
Fats: 15 g
Carbs: 30 g

119. Vegan Coconut Curry Lentil Soup

Yield: 4 servings   Cooking time: 40 min

INGREDIENTS

- 1 tablespoon coconut oil (15 ml)
- 1 onion, chopped
- 3 cloves garlic, minced
- 1 tablespoon grated ginger (15 g)
- 2 carrots, diced (150 g)
- 1 cup red lentils, rinsed (185 g)
- 4 cups vegetable broth (960 ml)
- 1 can (14 oz) coconut milk (400 ml)
- 2 tablespoons curry powder (30 g)
- Salt and pepper to taste
- Fresh cilantro for garnish (optional)

DIRECTIONS

In a large pot, heat the coconut oil over medium heat. Add the chopped onion and cook until softened, about 3-4 minutes.

Stir in the minced garlic and grated ginger, and cook for an additional 1-2 minutes.

Add the diced carrots and rinsed red lentils to the pot. Stir to combine.

Pour in the vegetable broth and coconut milk. Stir in the curry powder.

Bring the mixture to a boil, then reduce the heat to low and simmer for 20-25 minutes, or until the lentils are tender. Season with salt and pepper to taste.

Serve the vegan coconut curry lentil soup hot, garnished with fresh cilantro if desired.

Nutritional Information (Per Serving):
Calories 250 kcal
Proteins: 10g
Fats: 10g
Carbs: 35 g

120. Vegan Chickpea Salad Sandwiches

Yield: 4 servings   Cooking time: 15 min

INGREDIENTS

- 1 can (15 oz) chickpeas, drained and rinsed (425 g)
- 2 tablespoons vegan mayonnaise (30 g)
- 1 tablespoon Dijon mustard (15 g)
- 1 tablespoon lemon juice (15 ml)
- 1/4 cup finely chopped celery (40 g)
- 1/4 cup finely chopped red onion (40 g)
- Salt and pepper to taste
- 8 slices whole grain bread
- Lettuce leaves and sliced tomatoes for serving

DIRECTIONS

In a mixing bowl, mash the chickpeas with a fork or potato masher until they reach your desired consistency.

Add the vegan mayonnaise, Dijon mustard, lemon juice, chopped celery, and chopped red onion to the mashed chickpeas. Stir to combine.

Season the chickpea salad mixture with salt and pepper to taste.

Divide the chickpea salad evenly among 4 slices of whole grain bread.

Top each sandwich with lettuce leaves, sliced tomatoes, and the remaining slices of bread.

Serve the vegan chickpea salad sandwiches immediately, or wrap them tightly in parchment paper or plastic wrap for later.

Nutritional Information (Per Serving):
Calories: 280 kcal
Proteins: 10 g
Fats: 5 g
Carbs: 40 g

121. Cashew Milk Creamy Pasta Primavera

Yield: 4 servings   Cooking time: 30 min

INGREDIENTS
8 oz whole wheat pasta (225 g)
1 cup cashew milk (240 ml)
2 cups mixed vegetables (such as bell peppers, zucchini, cherry tomatoes) (300 g)
2 cloves garlic, minced
2 tablespoons olive oil (30 ml)
1/4 cup nutritional yeast (20 g)
1 tablespoon lemon juice (15 ml)
Salt and pepper to taste
Fresh basil leaves for garnish (optional)

DIRECTIONS
Cook the whole wheat pasta according to the package instructions. Drain and set aside.

In a large skillet, heat the olive oil over medium heat. Add the minced garlic and sauté for 1-2 minutes until fragrant.

Add the mixed vegetables to the skillet and cook until they are tender yet still crisp, about 5-7 minutes.

Pour in the cashew milk and nutritional yeast, stirring to combine.

Add the cooked pasta to the skillet, tossing to coat it evenly with the creamy sauce.

Stir in the lemon juice and season with salt and pepper to taste.

Serve the cashew milk creamy pasta primavera hot, garnished with fresh basil leaves if desired.

Nutritional Information (Per Serving):
Calories: 300 kcal
Proteins: 10 g
Fats: 10 g
Carbs: 40 g

122. Vegan Creamy Tomato Basil Soup

Yield: 4 servings   Cooking time: 40 min

INGREDIENTS
1 tablespoon olive oil (15 ml)
1 onion, chopped
2 cloves garlic, minced
1 can (28 oz) diced tomatoes (800 g)
2 cups vegetable broth (480 ml)
1/4 cup fresh basil leaves, chopped (10 g)
1/2 cup canned coconut milk (120 ml)
Salt and pepper to taste

DIRECTIONS
Heat the olive oil in a large pot over medium heat. Add the chopped onion and minced garlic, and cook until softened, about 5 minutes.

Add the diced tomatoes (with their juices) and vegetable broth to the pot. Bring to a simmer and cook for 20-25 minutes.

Using an immersion blender, blend the soup until smooth. Alternatively, transfer the soup to a blender and blend in batches until smooth, then return to the pot.

Stir in the chopped fresh basil and canned coconut milk. Season with salt and pepper to taste.

Simmer for an additional 5 minutes to allow the flavors to meld.

Serve the vegan creamy tomato basil soup hot, garnished with additional basil leaves if desired.

Nutritional Information (Per Serving):
Calories: 200 kcal
Proteins: 3 g
Fats: 10 g
Carbs: 15 g

123. Dairy-Free Pumpkin Coconut Soup

Yield: 4 servings   Cooking time: 40 min

INGREDIENTS

- 1 tablespoon coconut oil (15 ml)
- 1 onion, chopped
- 2 cloves garlic, minced
- 1 can (15 oz) pumpkin puree (425 g)
- 2 cups vegetable broth (480 ml)
- 1 can (13.5 oz) coconut milk (400 ml)
- 1 tablespoon maple syrup (15 ml)
- 1 teaspoon ground cinnamon (5 g)
- 1/2 teaspoon ground nutmeg (2.5 g)
- Salt and pepper to taste
- Fresh parsley for garnish (optional)

DIRECTIONS

In a large pot, heat the coconut oil over medium heat. Add the chopped onion and minced garlic, and cook until softened, about 5 minutes.

Add the pumpkin puree, vegetable broth, coconut milk, maple syrup, ground cinnamon, and ground nutmeg to the pot. Stir to combine.

Bring the mixture to a simmer and cook for 20-25 minutes, stirring occasionally.

Season the soup with salt and pepper to taste.

Remove from heat and let cool slightly before serving.

Serve the dairy-free pumpkin coconut soup hot, garnished with fresh parsley if desired.

Nutritional Information (Per Serving):
Calories: 220 kcal
Proteins: 3 g
Fats: 16 g
Carbs: 25 g

124. Vegan Cashew Cheese Stuffed Mushrooms

Yield: 4 servings   Cooking time: 30 min

INGREDIENTS

- 12 large mushrooms
- 1 cup raw cashews, soaked in water for 4 hours or overnight (150 g)
- 2 tablespoons nutritional yeast (15 g)
- 1 tablespoon lemon juice (15 ml)
- 1 clove garlic, minced
- 1/2 teaspoon onion powder (2.5 g)
- Salt and pepper to taste
- Fresh parsley for garnish (optional)

DIRECTIONS

Preheat the oven to 375°F (190°C). Lightly grease a baking dish with olive oil or non-stick cooking spray.

Remove the stems from the mushrooms and set aside. Place the mushroom caps in the prepared baking dish, gill side up.

In a food processor or blender, combine the soaked cashews, nutritional yeast, lemon juice, minced garlic, onion powder, salt, and pepper. Blend until smooth and creamy, adding a tablespoon of water at a time if needed to achieve the desired consistency.

Spoon the cashew cheese mixture into the mushroom caps, filling each one generously.

Bake in the preheated oven for 20-25 minutes, or until the mushrooms are tender and the filling is golden brown.

Remove from the oven and let cool slightly before serving.

Serve the vegan cashew cheese stuffed mushrooms warm, garnished with fresh parsley if desired.

Nutritional Information (Per Serving):
Calories: 150 kcal
Proteins: 7 g
Fats: 10 g
Carbs: 7 g

125. Coconut Milk Green Curry Stir-Fry

Yield: 4 servings   Cooking time: 30 min

INGREDIENTS

- 1 tablespoon coconut oil (15 ml)
- 1 onion, thinly sliced, 2 cloves garlic, minced
- 1 bell pepper, thinly sliced
- 2 cups mixed vegetables (such as broccoli, carrots, and snap peas) (300 g)
- 1 can (14 oz) coconut milk (400 ml)
- 2 tablespoons green curry paste (30 g)
- 1 tablespoon soy sauce or tamari (15 ml)
- 1 tablespoon maple syrup or coconut sugar (15 ml)
- Salt and pepper to taste
- Fresh cilantro for garnish (optional)
- Cooked rice or quinoa for serving

Nutritional Information (Per Serving):
Calories: 300 kcal
Proteins: 10 g
Fats: 10 g
Carbs: 40 g

DIRECTIONS

In a large skillet or wok, heat the coconut oil over medium heat. Add the sliced onion and minced garlic, and cook until softened, about 3-4 minutes.

Add the sliced bell pepper and mixed vegetables to the skillet. Stir-fry for another 5-6 minutes, or until the vegetables are tender-crisp.

In a small bowl, whisk together the coconut milk, green curry paste, soy sauce or tamari, and maple syrup or coconut sugar.

Pour the coconut milk mixture over the vegetables in the skillet. Stir to combine.

Bring the mixture to a simmer and cook for 5-7 minutes, stirring occasionally, until the sauce has thickened slightly.

Season with salt and pepper to taste.

Remove from heat and let cool slightly before serving.

Serve the coconut milk green curry stir-fry hot, garnished with fresh cilantro if desired. Serve over cooked rice or quinoa.

Chapter 10: Healthy Dessert Delights

Welcome to "Healthy Dessert Delights"! In this chapter, we present a collection of mouthwatering dessert recipes that are not only delicious but also nutritious. Indulge in guilt-free treats made with wholesome ingredients, perfect for satisfying your sweet cravings while nourishing your body. From fruity delights to decadent chocolate creations, these recipes are designed to delight your taste buds while promoting a balanced lifestyle. Get ready to indulge in desserts that are as good for you as they are delicious!

126. Berry Chia Seed Pudding

Yield: 2 servings   Cooking time: 5 min

INGREDIENTS
1/4 cup (40g) chia seeds
1 cup (240ml) almond milk
1 tablespoon (15ml) honey or maple syrup
1/2 teaspoon vanilla extract
1/2 cup (75g) mixed berries (blueberries, raspberries, strawberries)

DIRECTIONS
In a bowl, mix chia seeds, almond milk, honey or maple syrup, and vanilla extract.
Let it sit for about 5 minutes, then stir again to prevent clumps.
Cover and refrigerate overnight or for at least 2 hours.
Before serving, layer the chia pudding with mixed berries.
Enjoy your delicious and nutritious berry chia seed pudding!

Nutritional Information (Per Serving):
Calories : 150 kcal
Proteins: 3 g
Fats: 6 g
Carbs: 22 g

127. Avocado Chocolate Mousse

Yield: 4 servings   Cooking time: 10 min

INGREDIENTS

2 ripe avocados
1/4 cup (20g) cocoa powder
1/4 cup (60ml) maple syrup or honey
1 teaspoon vanilla extract
Pinch of salt
Optional toppings: shaved dark chocolate, berries, chopped nuts

DIRECTIONS

Scoop the flesh out of the avocados and place it in a food processor.

Add cocoa powder, maple syrup or honey, vanilla extract, and salt.

Blend until smooth and creamy, scraping down the sides as needed.

Transfer the mousse to serving cups or bowls.

Refrigerate for at least 30 minutes before serving.

Garnish with shaved dark chocolate, berries, or chopped nuts if desired.

Enjoy your decadent and healthy avocado chocolate mousse!

Nutritional Information (Per Serving):
Calories: 180 kcal
Proteins: 2 g
Fats: 11 g
Carbs: 21 g

128. Banana Oat Cookies

Yield: 8 servings   Cooking time: 30 min

INGREDIENTS

2 ripe bananas
1 cup (80g) rolled oats
1/4 cup (30g) chopped nuts or seeds (such as walnuts, almonds, or pumpkin seeds)
1/4 cup (40g) raisins or dried cranberries (optional)
1/2 teaspoon cinnamon (optional)
Pinch of salt

DIRECTIONS

Preheat your oven to 350°F (175°C). Line a baking sheet with parchment paper.

In a mixing bowl, mash the ripe bananas with a fork until smooth.

Add rolled oats, chopped nuts or seeds, raisins or dried cranberries (if using), cinnamon (if using), and a pinch of salt. Stir until well combined.

Drop spoonfuls of the mixture onto the prepared baking sheet, shaping them into cookies with the back of the spoon.

Bake for 12-15 minutes, or until the cookies are golden brown around the edges.

Remove from the oven and let them cool on the baking sheet for a few minutes before transferring to a wire rack to cool completely.

Enjoy your healthy and delicious banana oat cookies as a guilt-free treat!

Nutritional Information (Per Serving):
Calories: 150 kcal
Proteins: 7 g
Fats: 10 g
Carbs: 7 g

129. Coconut Yogurt Parfait with Fresh Fruit

Yield: 1 servings   Cooking time: 5 min

INGREDIENTS
- 1 cup (240g) coconut yogurt
- 1/2 cup (80g) mixed fresh fruit (such as berries, sliced bananas, diced mango)
- 2 tablespoons (30g) granola
- Optional toppings: shredded coconut, chopped nuts, honey or maple syrup

DIRECTIONS
In a serving glass or bowl, layer coconut yogurt with mixed fresh fruit.

Sprinkle granola over the fruit layer.

Repeat the layers until the glass or bowl is filled.

Garnish with optional toppings such as shredded coconut, chopped nuts, and a drizzle of honey or maple syrup.

Serve immediately and enjoy your refreshing coconut yogurt parfait with fresh fruit!

Nutritional Information (Per Serving):
Calories: 250 kcal
Proteins: 6 g
Fats: 8 g
Carbs: 40 g

130. Almond Butter Energy Balls

Yield: 12 servings   Cooking time: 40 min

INGREDIENTS
- 1 cup (90g) rolled oats
- 1/2 cup (120g) almond butter
- 1/4 cup (60ml) honey or maple syrup
- 1/4 cup (40g) chopped almonds
- 1/4 cup (40g) dried cranberries or raisins
- 1 tablespoon (15g) chia seeds
- Pinch of salt

DIRECTIONS
In a mixing bowl, combine rolled oats, almond butter, honey or maple syrup, chopped almonds, dried cranberries or raisins, chia seeds, and a pinch of salt.

Mix well until the ingredients are evenly combined.

Roll the mixture into bite-sized balls using your hands.

Place the energy balls on a plate or baking sheet lined with parchment paper.

Refrigerate for at least 30 minutes to firm up.

Once firm, transfer the energy balls to an airtight container and store in the refrigerator.

Enjoy these almond butter energy balls as a nutritious snack on the go!

Nutritional Information (Per Serving):
Calories: 120 kcal
Proteins: 3 g
Fats: 7 g
Carbs: 13 g

131. Baked Apples with Cinnamon and Walnuts

Yield: 2 servings   Cooking time: 35 min

INGREDIENTS

2 apples
2 tablespoons (30g) chopped walnuts
1 tablespoon (15ml) honey or maple syrup
1/2 teaspoon cinnamon
Pinch of nutmeg (optional)
Vanilla Greek yogurt or coconut yogurt for serving (optional)

DIRECTIONS

Preheat your oven to 375°F (190°C).
Core the apples and cut them in half horizontally.
Place the apple halves cut-side up in a baking dish.
In a small bowl, mix together chopped walnuts, honey or maple syrup, cinnamon, and nutmeg (if using).
Spoon the walnut mixture into the center of each apple half.
Cover the baking dish with foil and bake for 20-25 minutes, or until the apples are tender.
Serve the baked apples warm, optionally with a dollop of vanilla Greek yogurt or coconut yogurt.
Enjoy your cozy and nutritious baked apples with cinnamon and walnuts!

Nutritional Information (Per Serving):
Calories: 125 kcal
Proteins: 5 g
Fats: 2 g
Carbs: 28 g

132. Mango Coconut Nice Cream

Yield: 2 servings   Cooking time: 5 min + 1-2 hours

INGREDIENTS

2 ripe bananas, sliced and frozen
1 cup (150g) diced ripe mango, frozen
1/4 cup (60ml) coconut milk
1 tablespoon (15ml) honey or maple syrup (optional)
Shredded coconut and sliced mango for topping (optional)

DIRECTIONS

In a food processor or blender, combine frozen banana slices, frozen diced mango, coconut milk, and honey or maple syrup if using.
Blend until smooth and creamy, scraping down the sides as needed.
Transfer the nice cream to a freezer-safe container and freeze for about 1-2 hours to firm up.
Once firm, scoop the nice cream into serving bowls.
Garnish with shredded coconut and sliced mango if desired.
Serve immediately and enjoy your refreshing mango coconut nice cream!

Nutritional Information (Per Serving):
Calories: 200 kcal
Proteins: 2 g
Fats: 4 g
Carbs: 42 g

133. Chocolate Covered Strawberries

Yield: 2 servings   Cooking time: 30 min

INGREDIENTS

200g strawberries
100g dark chocolate chips
1 teaspoon coconut oil

DIRECTIONS

Wash and pat dry the strawberries, leaving the stems intact.

In a microwave-safe bowl, melt the dark chocolate chips and coconut oil in 30-second intervals, stirring between each interval until smooth.

Dip each strawberry into the melted chocolate mixture, coating it evenly.

Place the chocolate-covered strawberries on a parchment-lined baking sheet.

Refrigerate for about 15-20 minutes, or until the chocolate hardens.

Serve and enjoy these decadent chocolate-covered strawberries as a delightful dessert or snack!

Nutritional Information (Per Serving):
Calories: 150 kcal
Proteins: 2 g
Fats: 7 g
Carbs: 20 g

---

134. Quinoa Coconut Macaroons

Yield: 8 servings   Cooking time: 30 min

INGREDIENTS

1 cup (185g) cooked quinoa, cooled
1/2 cup (40g) unsweetened shredded coconut
1/4 cup (60ml) honey or maple syrup
1/4 cup (60ml) coconut oil, melted
1 teaspoon vanilla extract
Pinch of salt

DIRECTIONS

Preheat your oven to 350°F (175°C) and line a baking sheet with parchment paper.

In a large mixing bowl, combine cooked quinoa, shredded coconut, honey or maple syrup, melted coconut oil, vanilla extract, and a pinch of salt.

Mix well until all ingredients are thoroughly combined.

Using a tablespoon, scoop the mixture and shape it into balls, then flatten slightly to form macaroon shapes.

Place the macaroons on the prepared baking sheet.

Bake for 15-20 minutes, or until the edges are golden brown.

Remove from the oven and let cool completely before serving.

Enjoy these delicious quinoa coconut macaroons as a nutritious gluten-free dessert or snack!

Nutritional Information (Per Serving):
Calories: 120 kcal
Proteins: 1 g
Fats: 7 g
Carbs: 14 g

135. Pumpkin Spice Baked Oatmeal Bars

Yield: 6 servings   Cooking time: 40 min

INGREDIENTS
- 2 cups (160g) rolled oats
- 1/2 cup (120ml) almond milk
- 1/2 cup (120g) pumpkin puree
- 1/4 cup (60ml) maple syrup
- 1 teaspoon pumpkin pie spice
- 1/4 cup (40g) raisins or dried cranberries
- 1/4 cup (30g) chopped walnuts (optional)

DIRECTIONS
Preheat your oven to 350°F (175°C) and grease a baking dish with coconut oil or line it with parchment paper.

In a mixing bowl, combine rolled oats, almond milk, pumpkin puree, maple syrup, pumpkin pie spice, raisins or dried cranberries, and chopped walnuts if using.

Mix well until all ingredients are evenly combined.

Transfer the mixture to the prepared baking dish and spread it out evenly.

Bake for 25-30 minutes, or until the top is golden brown and firm to the touch.

Remove from the oven and let cool before slicing into bars.

Serve and enjoy these pumpkin spice baked oatmeal bars as a wholesome and flavorful treat!

Nutritional Information (Per Serving):
Calories: 180 kcal
Proteins: 4 g
Fats: 3 g
Carbs: 34 g

---

136. Raspberry Almond Flour Cake

Yield: 8 servings   Cooking time: 40 min

INGREDIENTS
- 1 1/2 cups (150g) almond flour
- 1/4 cup (30g) coconut flour
- 1 teaspoon baking powder
- 1/4 teaspoon salt
- 1/2 cup (120ml) coconut oil, melted
- 1/2 cup (120ml) honey or maple syrup
- 3 large eggs
- 1 teaspoon vanilla extract
- 1 cup (150g) fresh raspberries

DIRECTIONS
Preheat your oven to 350°F (175°C). Grease a cake pan with coconut oil or line it with parchment paper.

In a mixing bowl, whisk together almond flour, coconut flour, baking powder, and salt.

In another bowl, whisk together melted coconut oil, honey or maple syrup, eggs, and vanilla extract.

Gradually add the wet ingredients to the dry ingredients, mixing until well combined.

Gently fold in the fresh raspberries.

Pour the batter into the prepared cake pan and spread it out evenly.

Bake for 25-30 minutes, or until a toothpick inserted into the center comes out clean.

Allow the cake to cool before slicing and serving.

Enjoy a slice of this delicious raspberry almond flour cake as a delightful gluten-free dessert or snack!

Nutritional Information (Per Serving):
Calories: 250 kcal
Proteins: 6 g
Fats: 17 g
Carbs: 20 g

137. Lemon Poppy Seed Muffins with Greek Yogurt Glaze

Yield: 6 servings   Cooking time: 40 min

INGREDIENTS

1 1/2 cups (180g) almond flour
1/4 cup (30g) coconut flour
1/4 cup (60ml) coconut oil, melted
1/4 cup (60ml) honey or maple syrup
3 large eggs, Juice and zest of 1 lemon
1 tablespoon poppy seeds
1/2 teaspoon baking soda, 1/4 teaspoon salt
For the glaze:
1/2 cup (120g) Greek yogurt
1 tablespoon honey or maple syrup
Juice of 1/2 lemon

Nutritional Information
(Per Serving):
Calories: 180 kcal
Proteins: 5 g
Fats: 12 g
Carbs: 15 g

DIRECTIONS

Preheat your oven to 350°F (175°C). Line a muffin tin with paper liners. In a large bowl, whisk together almond flour, coconut flour, baking soda, salt, and poppy seeds.
In another bowl, whisk together melted coconut oil, honey or maple syrup, eggs, lemon juice, and lemon zest.
Gradually add the wet ingredients to the dry ingredients, mixing until well combined. Divide the batter evenly among the muffin cups. Bake for 20-25 minutes, or until a toothpick inserted into the center comes out clean.
Allow the muffins to cool in the tin for 5 minutes, then transfer them to a wire rack to cool completely.
In a small bowl, whisk together Greek yogurt, honey or maple syrup, and lemon juice to make the glaze.
Drizzle the glaze over the cooled muffins.
Enjoy these lemon poppy seed muffins with Greek yogurt glaze as a delicious and nutritious breakfast or snack!

138. Peach Crisp with Almond Flour Topping

Yield: 6 servings   Cooking time: 45 min

INGREDIENTS

4 cups (600g) sliced peaches
1 tablespoon (15ml) lemon juice
1/4 cup (30g) coconut sugar
1/2 teaspoon ground cinnamon
1/4 teaspoon ground nutmeg
For the topping:
1 cup (100g) almond flour
1/4 cup (20g) rolled oats
1/4 cup (30g) chopped almonds
2 tablespoons (30ml) maple syrup
2 tablespoons (30g) coconut oil, melted

Nutritional Information
(Per Serving):
Calories: 220 kcal
Proteins: 4 g
Fats: 15 g
Carbs: 20 g

DIRECTIONS

Preheat your oven to 350°F (175°C). Grease a baking dish with coconut oil.
In a large bowl, toss the sliced peaches with lemon juice, coconut sugar, cinnamon, and nutmeg. Transfer the peach mixture to the prepared baking dish.
In another bowl, combine almond flour, rolled oats, chopped almonds, maple syrup, melted coconut oil, and a pinch of salt. Mix until crumbly.
Sprinkle the almond flour topping evenly over the peaches.
Bake for 25-30 minutes, or until the topping is golden brown and the peaches are bubbling.
Remove from the oven and let cool slightly before serving.
Serve warm with a scoop of vanilla ice cream or coconut whipped cream, if desired.
Enjoy this delicious peach crisp with almond flour topping as a delightful dessert!

139. Kiwi Lime Sorbet

Yield: 4 servings Cooking time: 10 min + 2-3 hours

INGREDIENTS
4 ripe kiwis, peeled and chopped
Juice and zest of 2 limes
1/4 cup (60ml) water
2-3 tablespoons (30-45ml) honey or maple syrup (optional)

DIRECTIONS
Place the chopped kiwis, lime juice, lime zest, water, and honey or maple syrup (if using) in a blender.
Blend until smooth.
Pour the mixture into a shallow dish or baking pan.
Freeze for 2-3 hours, stirring every 30 minutes with a fork to break up any ice crystals.
Once the sorbet is firm and scoopable, transfer it to a container and freeze until ready to serve.
Serve the kiwi lime sorbet in chilled bowls or glasses.
Garnish with fresh kiwi slices or lime zest, if desired.
Enjoy this refreshing and tangy kiwi lime sorbet on a hot day!

Nutritional Information (Per Serving):
Calories: 80 kcal
Proteins: 1 g
Fats: 0 g
Carbs: 20 g

140. Carrot Cake Energy Bites

Yield: 12 servings Cooking time: 40 min

INGREDIENTS
1 cup (90g) rolled oats
1/2 cup (50g) shredded carrots
1/4 cup (40g) chopped walnuts
1/4 cup (40g) raisins
2 tablespoons (30g) almond butter
2 tablespoons (30ml) maple syrup
1/2 teaspoon ground cinnamon
Pinch of nutmeg
Pinch of salt

DIRECTIONS
In a food processor, combine rolled oats, shredded carrots, chopped walnuts, raisins, almond butter, maple syrup, cinnamon, nutmeg, and a pinch of salt.
Pulse until the mixture comes together and forms a dough-like consistency.
Roll the mixture into bite-sized balls using your hands.
Place the energy bites on a plate or baking sheet lined with parchment paper.
Refrigerate for at least 30 minutes to firm up.
Once firm, transfer the energy bites to an airtight container and store in the refrigerator.
Enjoy these carrot cake energy bites as a nutritious snack on the go!

Nutritional Information (Per Serving):
Calories: 80 kcal
Proteins: 2 g
Fats: 3 g
Carbs: 12 g

141. Chocolate Avocado Pudding

Yield: 4 servings Cooking time: 40 min

INGREDIENTS

2 ripe avocados
1/4 cup (25g) unsweetened cocoa powder
1/4 cup (60ml) maple syrup or honey
1/4 cup (60ml) almond milk or coconut milk
1 teaspoon vanilla extract
Pinch of salt

Optional toppings: sliced strawberries, chopped nuts, shredded coconut

Nutritional Information (Per Serving):
Calories: 80 kcal
Proteins: 1 g
Fats: 0 g
Carbs: 20 g

DIRECTIONS

Cut the avocados in half, remove the pits, and scoop the flesh into a food processor or blender.

Add cocoa powder, maple syrup or honey, almond milk or coconut milk, vanilla extract, and a pinch of salt to the blender. Blend until the mixture is smooth and creamy, scraping down the sides as needed to ensure everything is well incorporated. Taste the pudding and adjust sweetness if necessary by adding more maple syrup or honey.

Transfer the chocolate avocado pudding to serving bowls or glasses.

Chill in the refrigerator for at least 30 minutes before serving to allow it to firm up slightly.

Once chilled, garnish with sliced strawberries, chopped nuts, or shredded coconut if desired.

Serve and enjoy this rich and creamy chocolate avocado pudding as a healthy dessert or snack!

Chapter 11: Aquatic Delights: Refreshing Recipes

"Welcome to the chapter on crafting infused water! Here, you'll discover exciting recipes for creating water infused with fruits, herbs, and other ingredients. These refreshing and nutritious beverages not only quench your thirst but also energize you for the day ahead. Let's explore the options together and savor the refreshing flavors of infused water!"

142. Lemon and Mint Infused Water

Yield: 4 servings   Preparation Time: 5 min

INGREDIENTS
1 lemon, thinly sliced
Handful of fresh mint leaves
1 liter of water
Ice cubes (optional)

DIRECTIONS
Wash the lemon thoroughly under running water to remove any dirt or residue. Slice the lemon thinly.
Wash the fresh mint leaves and gently bruise them with your fingers to release their flavor.
In a large pitcher, add the lemon slices and mint leaves.
Fill the pitcher with 1 liter of water. You can use filtered water or tap water.
Stir the ingredients gently to distribute the flavors.
Cover the pitcher and refrigerate for at least 1 hour to allow the flavors to infuse.
Once chilled, serve the lemon and mint infused water over ice cubes, if desired.
You can refill the pitcher with water a couple of times before needing to replace the lemon and mint.
Enjoy this refreshing and hydrating lemon and mint infused water as a healthy beverage option!

143. Cucumber Mint Detox Water

Yield: 4 servings   Preparation Time: 5 min

INGREDIENTS

- 1 cucumber, sliced
- 10-12 fresh mint leaves
- 1 lemon, sliced
- 2 liters (8 cups) of water
- Ice cubes (optional)

DIRECTIONS

In a large pitcher, combine the sliced cucumber, fresh mint leaves, and lemon slices.
Fill the pitcher with 2 liters (8 cups) of water.
Stir the ingredients gently to combine.
Refrigerate the detox water for at least 2 hours to allow the flavors to infuse.
Serve the cucumber mint detox water chilled, adding ice cubes if desired.

144. Strawberry Basil Infusion

Yield: 8 servings   Preparation Time: 5 min

INGREDIENTS

- 1 cup fresh strawberries, hulled and halved
- 10-12 fresh basil leaves
- 1 lemon, thinly sliced
- 2 liters (8 cups) of water
- Ice cubes (optional)

DIRECTIONS

In a large pitcher, combine the fresh strawberries, basil leaves, and lemon slices.
Fill the pitcher with 2 liters (8 cups) of water.
Stir gently to mix the ingredients.
Refrigerate the infusion for at least 1-2 hours to allow the flavors to meld.
Serve the strawberry basil infusion chilled, adding ice cubes if desired.

145. Orange Ginger Splash

Yield: 4 servings　　　　Preparation Time: 5 min

INGREDIENTS

2 oranges, sliced
1-inch piece of ginger, peeled and thinly sliced
1 lemon, sliced
2 liters (8 cups) of water
Ice cubes (optional)

DIRECTIONS

In a large pitcher, combine the sliced oranges, ginger slices, and lemon slices.
Fill the pitcher with 2 liters (8 cups) of water.
Stir gently to mix the ingredients.
Refrigerate the infusion for at least 1-2 hours to allow the flavors to meld.
Serve the orange ginger splash chilled, adding ice cubes if desired.

146. Blueberry Lavender Elixir

Yield: 8 servings　　　　Preparation Time: 5 min

INGREDIENTS

2 cups fresh blueberries
1 tablespoon dried lavender buds
1 lemon, sliced
2 liters (8 cups) water
Ice cubes (optional)

DIRECTIONS

In a large pitcher, combine the fresh blueberries and dried lavender buds.
Add the sliced lemon to the pitcher.
Fill the pitcher with 2 liters (8 cups) of water.
Stir gently to mix the ingredients.
Refrigerate the elixir for at least 1-2 hours to allow the flavors to infuse.
Serve the blueberry lavender elixir chilled, adding ice cubes if desired.

147. Pineapple Coconut Refresher

Yield: 4 servings   Preparation Time: 5 min

INGREDIENTS

2 cups fresh pineapple chunks
1 cup coconut water
1 tablespoon lime juice
Ice cubes (optional)
Pineapple slices and mint leaves for garnish (optional)

DIRECTIONS

In a blender, combine the fresh pineapple chunks, coconut water, and lime juice.

Blend until smooth and well combined.

If desired, add ice cubes to the blender and blend again until the mixture is chilled and frothy.

Pour the pineapple coconut refresher into glasses.

Garnish each glass with a slice of pineapple and a sprig of mint, if desired.

Serve immediately and enjoy the refreshing tropical drink!

148. Raspberry Rosemary Infusion

Yield: 4 servings   Preparation Time: 5 min

INGREDIENTS

1 cup fresh raspberries
2 sprigs fresh rosemary
4 cups water
Ice cubes (optional)
Fresh raspberries and rosemary sprigs for garnish (optional)

DIRECTIONS

In a large pitcher, combine the fresh raspberries and rosemary sprigs.

Fill the pitcher with water.

Stir gently to slightly crush the raspberries and release the flavor of the rosemary.

Cover the pitcher and refrigerate for at least 1 hour to allow the flavors to infuse.

Serve the raspberry rosemary infusion over ice cubes, if desired.

Garnish each glass with fresh raspberries and a sprig of rosemary, if desired.

Enjoy this refreshing and aromatic drink!

149. Kiwi Strawberry Splash

Yield: 4 servings   Preparation Time: 10 min

INGREDIENTS

2 kiwis, peeled and sliced
1 cup sliced strawberries
4 cups cold water
Ice cubes (optional)
Kiwi slices and strawberry halves for garnish (optional)

DIRECTIONS

In a large pitcher, combine the sliced kiwis and strawberries.
Pour cold water over the fruit mixture.
Stir well to combine.
Refrigerate the kiwi strawberry splash for at least 1 hour to allow the flavors to meld.
Serve the splash over ice cubes, if desired.
Garnish each glass with a slice of kiwi and a strawberry half, if desired.
Enjoy this delightful and refreshing drink!

150. Peach Thyme Hydration

Yield: 4 servings   Preparation Time: 10 min

INGREDIENTS

2 ripe peaches, pitted and sliced
4-6 sprigs fresh thyme
4 cups cold water
Ice cubes (optional)
Peach slices and thyme sprigs for garnish (optional)

DIRECTIONS

In a large pitcher, combine the sliced peaches and fresh thyme sprigs.
Pour cold water over the peach and thyme mixture.
Stir gently to distribute the flavors.
Refrigerate the peach thyme hydration for at least 1 hour to infuse the water with flavor.
Serve the infused water over ice cubes, if desired.
Garnish each glass with a peach slice and a sprig of thyme, if desired.
Enjoy this refreshing and aromatic drink!

151. Cherry Vanilla Bliss

Yield: 4 servings   Preparation Time: 10 min

INGREDIENTS

2 cups fresh cherries, pitted
1 vanilla bean pod, split lengthwise
4 cups cold water
Ice cubes (optional)
Fresh cherries and vanilla bean for garnish (optional)

DIRECTIONS

Place the pitted cherries in a large pitcher.
Scrape the seeds from the split vanilla bean pod and add both the seeds and the pod to the pitcher with the cherries.
Pour cold water over the cherry and vanilla mixture.
Stir gently to combine the ingredients.
Refrigerate the cherry vanilla bliss for at least 1 hour to allow the flavors to infuse.
Serve the infused water over ice cubes, if desired.
Garnish each glass with a fresh cherry and a piece of vanilla bean, if desired.
Enjoy this delightful and fragrant beverage!

152. Peach Thyme Hydration

Yield: 4 servings   Preparation Time: 10 min

INGREDIENTS

2 ripe peaches, pitted and sliced
4-6 sprigs fresh thyme
4 cups cold water
Ice cubes (optional)
Peach slices and thyme sprigs for garnish (optional)

DIRECTIONS

In a large pitcher, combine the sliced peaches and fresh thyme sprigs.
Pour cold water over the peach and thyme mixture.
Stir gently to distribute the flavors.
Refrigerate the peach thyme hydration for at least 1 hour to infuse the water with flavor.
Serve the infused water over ice cubes, if desired.
Garnish each glass with a peach slice and a sprig of thyme, if desired.
Enjoy this refreshing and aromatic drink!

153. Mango Pineapple Paradise

Yield: 4 servings　　　　Preparation Time: 10 min

INGREDIENTS

1 ripe mango, peeled, pitted, and diced
1 cup fresh pineapple chunks
4 cups cold water
Ice cubes (optional)
Fresh mint leaves for garnish (optional)

DIRECTIONS

In a large pitcher, combine the diced mango and pineapple chunks.
Pour cold water over the fruit mixture.
Stir gently to combine.
Refrigerate the infused water for at least 1 hour to allow the flavors to meld.
Serve the Mango Pineapple Paradise over ice cubes, if desired.
Garnish each glass with fresh mint leaves for an extra burst of flavor.
Enjoy this tropical and refreshing beverage!

154. Blackberry Sage Infused Water

Yield: 4 servings　　　　Preparation Time: 10 min

INGREDIENTS

1 cup fresh blackberries
4-5 fresh sage leaves
4 cups cold water
Ice cubes (optional)

DIRECTIONS

Rinse the blackberries and sage leaves under cold water.
In a large pitcher, add the blackberries and sage leaves.
Pour cold water over the ingredients in the pitcher.
Use a muddler or the back of a spoon to gently press on the blackberries and sage leaves to release their flavors.
Stir the mixture gently to combine.
Refrigerate the infused water for at least 1-2 hours to allow the flavors to infuse.
Before serving, you can strain the water to remove the blackberries and sage leaves if desired, or leave them in for added flavor and visual appeal.
Serve the blackberry sage infused water over ice cubes if desired.
Enjoy this refreshing and flavorful beverage!

155. Apple Cinnamon Quencher

Yield: 4 servings Preparation Time: 10 min

INGREDIENTS
- 1 medium apple, thinly sliced
- 2 cinnamon sticks
- 4 cups cold water
- Ice cubes (optional)

DIRECTIONS
Wash the apple thoroughly and cut it into thin slices.
In a large pitcher, add the apple slices and cinnamon sticks.
Pour cold water into the pitcher, covering the apple slices and cinnamon sticks.
Stir the mixture gently to combine.
Refrigerate the infused water for at least 1-2 hours to allow the flavors to infuse.
Before serving, you can remove the apple slices and cinnamon sticks if desired, or leave them in for added flavor and visual appeal.
Serve the apple cinnamon quencher over ice cubes if desired.
Enjoy this refreshing and fragrant beverage!

156. Raspberry Water Infusion

Yield: 4 servings Preparation Time: 5 min

INGREDIENTS
- 1 cup fresh raspberries
- 4 cups cold water
- Ice cubes (optional)
- Fresh mint leaves for garnish (optional)

DIRECTIONS
Rinse the raspberries under cold water and drain them.
In a large pitcher, add the raspberries.
Pour cold water into the pitcher, covering the raspberries.
Use a muddler or the back of a spoon to gently crush some of the raspberries to release their flavor.
Stir the mixture gently to distribute the raspberries evenly.
Refrigerate the infused water for at least 1-2 hours to allow the flavors to meld.
Before serving, you can strain out the raspberries if desired, or leave them in for a more intense flavor and visual appeal.
Serve the raspberry water infusion over ice cubes if desired.
Garnish with fresh mint leaves for an extra touch of freshness.
Enjoy this vibrant and refreshing raspberry-infused water!

Conclusion

In summary, adopting a clean eating approach is about making a lifestyle change that prioritizes nourishing your body with wholesome, nutrient-rich foods. Incorporating plenty of fresh vegetables and leafy greens provides essential vitamins, minerals, and antioxidants to support overall health.

Hydration is key. Drinking enough water helps regulate body temperature, aids digestion, flushes out toxins, and keeps skin healthy. Start your day with water to jumpstart metabolism and rehydrate after sleep.

Be mindful of sugar intake. Opt for natural sources of sweetness like fresh fruit or small amounts of honey instead of sugary snacks and beverages.

Intermittent fasting, with a 12-13 hour break between dinner and breakfast, can regulate hunger hormones, promote fat burning, and improve metabolic health.

Incorporating these principles can lead to increased energy, better digestion, improved mood, and weight management. Start small, focus on gradual changes, and celebrate successes.

Printed in Great Britain
by Amazon